Ready for Reading will help parents who are eager to share the joys of reading with their children. In addition to the warm and wonderful times that can be shared between a parent and child while reading, children's later academic success often depends on books playing a central role in their early lives.

The authors first provide clear, concise information about how children become readers and about the important contribution parents can make to their children's growth as readers. Then, the book goes on to provide "Book Shares" which feature 60 children's books to be shared with a child, and offers suggested activities for how to share these books. And accompanying each featured book is a list of recommended related books and poems—totaling more than 400 books and 400 poems—that have delighted children everywhere.

Features

* Sixty engaging and "kid-tested" Book Shares (book-sharing activities) give more than a year's worth of shared reading ideas. Some may be used any week of the year; others are most appropriate for certain times of the year.

* Included among the 60 Book Shares are eight which are offered to highlight special moments in a family's life, including the arrival of a new baby, a child's first sleepover, the first day in kindergarten, and a child's first stay in a hospital.

* Presents recommendations for more than 400 books and 400 poems for early readers.

* Convenient end-of-book indexes help parents quickly and easily l... that best suits a chil...

DB3701936?

Allyn and Bacon
Longwood Division
160 Gould Street
Needham Heights, MA 02494-2310
www.abacon.com

US $18.
Canada $26.

9 780205 287918

ISBN 0-205-28791-3

SO-CFB-825

0 76092 00520 9

90000

Cover Illustration: © Lance Hidy/SIS.

Ready for Reading

A Handbook for Parents of Preschoolers

✦ ✦ ✦

Ashley Bishop

California State University, Fullerton

Ruth Helen Yopp

California State University, Fullerton

Hallie Kay Yopp

California State University, Fullerton

Allyn and Bacon

Boston   London   Toronto   Sydney   Tokyo   Singapore

Senior Editor: Virginia C. Lanigan
Editorial Assistant: Bridget Keane
Editorial-Production Administrator: Annette Joseph
Editorial-Production Service: Holly Crawford
Design and Electronic Composition: Denise Hoffman
Composition Buyer: Linda Cox
Manufacturing Buyer: Suzanne Lareau
Cover Designer: Jenny Hart

Library of Congress Cataloging-in-Publication Data

Bishop, Ashley.
    Ready for reading : a handbook for parents of preschoolers /
Ashley Bishop, Ruth Helen Yopp, Hallie Kay Yopp.
        p.   cm.
    Includes bibliographical references and index.
    ISBN 0–205–28791–3
    1. Reading (Preschool) Handbooks, manuals, etc.   2. Reading—
Parent participation Handbooks, manuals, etc.   3. Children's
literature—Study and teaching (Preschool) Handbooks, manuals, etc.
4. Preschool children—Books and reading Handbooks, manuals, etc.
I. Yopp, Ruth Helen.   II. Yopp, Hallie Kay.   III. Title.
LB1140.5.R4B57   2000
372.4—dc21   99–12873
                                                          CIP

Printed in the United States of America

10 9 8 7 6   06 07 08 09

Photo Credits: Pages 8, 28, and 38, Will Faller.

*To our parents who made good literature a
pleasurable and important part of our lives,*

*To our children who have come to love and value
the world of books as much as we do,*

*And to all the parents and parent groups who
encouraged us to put our ideas in book form*

Contents

Introduction

Two bedrooms, midday.

Bedroom One has an aquarium filled with fish; a bulletin board hidden by art and writing activities; a bed covered with stuffed animals from children's literature, like Arthur, Curious George, and Clifford; a desk topped with paper, pencil, and crayons; and, most importantly, a bookcase brimming with books.

Bedroom Two is brimming with electrical toys: a TV, electronic games, a joystick, a VCR, a stereo, and an astonishing variety of remote controls.

The same two bedrooms, evening.

Bedroom One: A boy, a girl, a son, a daughter snuggles in bed with a stuffed bunny cradled in his or her arms. A parent sits on the bed and reads *Goodnight Moon* by Margaret Wise Brown. By the time the refrain "Good night to the old lady whispering 'hush'" is read, the child begins to understand, in a positive, nurturing environment, how books work and the wonders they contain. The child discovers that books are full of letters, sounds, words, ideas, information, and adventures. Even more importantly, the child comes to associate reading with the warm and wonderful times he or she has listening to mom or dad read as sleep gently arrives.

Bedroom Two has a harsh blue glow being chased, it seems, out the door by the even harsher sounds emanating from whatever electronic device is being played within. Battles are being waged, lives are being lost as the child, on the edge of his or her seat, is pulled deep into the action. Sleep, when it comes, is not gentle.

Now, a quick quiz. Close this book and your eyes, and picture your child's bedroom. What is in it? A bookcase? A TV? Both? Neither? Which bedroom will your child fall asleep in tonight? We are not opposed to everything that can be plugged in. Computers are wonderful and versatile tools. Watching television can be an enjoyable and informative activity for families to do together. Our concern is that Bedroom One is being rapidly replaced by Bedroom Two in homes from coast to coast. *Ready for Reading: A Handbook for Parents of Preschoolers* stresses that books must play a much more central role in the lives of children than electronic entertainment. Children's academic success often depends on it.

Ready for Reading will help parents who are eager to share the joys of reading with their children. In Part I of this book, we provide information about how children become readers and about the important contributions that parents can make to their children's growth as readers. In Part II, we feature 60 children's books to be shared with your child, and we offer suggestions for how to share these books. The book-sharing activities we describe are ones that develop in children those skills and insights necessary for success in reading. Accompanying each featured book is a list of recommended related books and poems, totaling more than 400 books and 400 poems that have delighted young children everywhere.

We suggest that you read to your child every day and that at least once each week you select one of the 60 featured books and engage in the accompanying activities. The first 52 will take you through a full year. Some may be used any week; others are most appropriate for certain times of the year. For example, *One Zillion Valentines* by Frank Modell is best shared the week of Valentine's Day. *The Carrot Seed* by Ruth Krauss is best shared in the spring or summer when you can engage in the recommended planting activity.

The eight additional featured books are offered to highlight special moments in your family's life. If you are expecting a new baby, you will want to share *The New Baby* by Mercer Mayer. If your son or daughter is going on his or her first sleepover, you will want to share *Ira Sleeps Over* by Bernard Waber. *Miss Bindergarten Gets Ready for Kindergarten* by Joseph Slate is ideal for the night before kindergarten entry.

The book-sharing activities have been tested on our own children, and we want to thank them for being such wonderful and willing volunteers. They, through their enthusiasm, sent us a clear message: This book works!

How children become ready for reading is often a process of mystery and magic for parents. We hope *Ready for Reading* takes the mystery out of the process and emphasizes the magic. We wish you, and your children, good reading.

Acknowledgments

Writing a book is not necessarily a pleasurable experience. This one was. There are many reasons why. The most important reason is that the subject of *Ready for Reading* is near and dear to our hearts. However, as near and dear as the topic is, without the continuous support, encouragement, and editorial advice of our spouses, *Ready for Reading* might never have come to fruition. So, Sue, Tom, and Bert, you have our heartfelt thanks.

We would also like to thank Amy Morgan for reading and responding to an early draft of *Ready for Reading*, Chad Bishop for contributing some of the photographs, and Jordan Fabish and Christie Whaling for their library and clerical assistance. We are grateful to Mitsuo Maeda and Lily Lui for sharing their expertise in Asian orthographies. The contributions of each of these individuals were invaluable.

We sincerely appreciate the time of Inge J. Carmola, P. David Pearson, Michigan State University, and Ellen M. Versprille for their reviews of *Ready for Reading*. Their insights were most helpful.

We thank our editor, Virginia Lanigan, for her guidance and support throughout the development of this book. In addition, we wish to acknowledge the contributions of Bridget Keane, Annette Joseph, Holly Crawford, and Denise Hoffman.

Part I

Ready for Reading

Chapter One

Learning to Read Begins at Home

*W*elcome to *Ready for Reading: A Handbook for Parents of Preschoolers.* Because you are reading this, the chances are that you or someone close to you has children. This book is important to both you and them. It is a book that celebrates children's literature and the role parents and caregivers can have in helping insure that their children experience success in the adventure called reading. It emphasizes that getting children ready for reading can be a warm and joyous process.

Ready for Reading strongly agrees with *Celebrating the National Reading Initiative* as it states,

> When "reading aloud" to children, parents offer more than the gift of a story. They give them warmth, safety, and love, which becomes strongly associated with stories and books. Memories of a father's voice or a mother's laughter are forever carried close to the heart. Children discover the wonder of words and probe the mystery of the world beyond their homes. They begin to experience the joy books offer. They want to read, too, just as their parents read. (1989, p. 2)

Preschoolers are at a very formative stage. How will they form the concepts that shape their lives? Will it be from a camel that smokes, a clown who loves fast food, and elves who make cookies or will it be from parents who share the love of reading and good literature with their children?

Ready for Reading is a book that says children's literature plays a positive and important role in young people's lives. Charlotte Huck, a leading authority on children's literature, and her colleagues tell us,

> All that people have ever thought, done, or dreamed lies waiting to be discovered in books. Literature begins with Mother Goose. It includes Sendak as well as Shakespeare, Milne as much as Milton, and Carroll before Camus. Children's literature is a part of the mainstream of all literature, whose source is life itself. (Huck, Hepler, & Hickman, 1987, p. 3)

Ready for Reading has a somber message as well. Keith Stanovich, a prolific researcher in the field of reading, describes the "Matthew Effect" (1993–94; 1986). He tells us the term derives from the Gospel according to Matthew: "For unto every one that hath shall be given, and he shall have abundance; but from him that hath not shall be taken away even that which he hath" (xxv:29). Stanovich is speaking in terms of early learning and early experiences. The achievement differences between children who enter school with certain insights and experiences and those who do not are magnified over time. The "rich get richer." In other words, children who come to school with certain insights and experiences make more and faster progress than their peers; there is a cumulative advantage to early success. Conversely, children who enter school without these insights and experiences typically make less and slower progress; there is a cumulative disadvantage to coming to school less well prepared.

Richard Allington and Sean Walmsley (1995), reading researchers, point to parents as key players in a child's literacy development. They assert that children must engage in literacy experiences before they come to school. Further, they claim that every child who participates in rich literacy experiences before entering school will be a child who is more likely to escape the fate of early failure in learning to read and of long-term difficulties with literacy learning.

The report of the Committee on the Prevention of Reading Difficulties in Young Children, funded by the National Academy of Sciences and the U.S. Department of Education, states, "It is clear from the research on emergent literacy that important experiences related to reading begin very early in life" (Snow, Burns, & Griffin, 1998, p. 317). There is abundant evidence, the report asserts, that what a child already knows, the experiences he or she already has had, profoundly impact reading progress in school. The obvious conclusion, then, is that the child's early environment—the home—plays a critical role in the ongoing reading development of that child. Those crucial years before children enter school significantly influence their understanding of what it means to read and their desire to read.

We hope you have been convinced that introducing and sharing good literature with children is not just kid's stuff! It can be the foundation for success in school and in life. In this light, *Ready for Reading* presents over 400 books, 400 poems, and 60 book-sharing activities that parents and caregivers can engage in with their children. We have not selected just any children's literature but literature that develops in children those insights and skills that research shows greatly enhance their chances for a successful beginning in reading. The books we have selected have four very important features that contribute to successful reading. The books you will be sharing with your children:

+ Allow them to develop the understanding that books are friends that can be trusted to entertain and inform for the rest of their lives.

+ Guide them to have a richer knowledge of the sounds in the words we speak.

+ Help them become familiar with the letters of the alphabet and their sounds.

+ Show them that books, and the sentences within them, work in familiar and predictable ways.

Ready for Reading is organized in the following way: Part I consists of four chapters. The rest of Chapter One describes the appearance of a home that produces children who enter school ready and eager to read. Chapter Two defines reading and discusses the roles of decoding and meaning. This chapter points out the value of using literature that focuses on important moments in children's lives. Chapter Three presents information about crucial abilities and insights that need to be developed in order for children to become successful readers. Chapter Four describes types of children's literature and provides suggestions for selecting and sharing children's literature. We hope that you carefully read all four chapters. They present an excellent foundation for the literature-sharing process and provide information that will be important throughout your child's school years. Part II of *Ready for Reading* offers 60 book-sharing experiences that parents and caregivers can use with their children.

The Home and Reading

Moving children toward reading can be a time-consuming task in a day and age in which time seems always in short supply. However, if you are taking the time to read this book, the chances are excellent that you are an individual who recognizes that no time is more valuable or precious than that spent with a child. The activities presented in *Ready for Reading* normally should not take more than 15 to 30 minutes a day. The invested time will pay incredible dividends in the future.

Becoming a Nation of Readers (1985), a document written when the National Academy of Education formed the Commission on Reading to investigate what needed to be done to produce a nation of readers, makes the following statements about parents and the importance of their making a commitment to guiding children to become ready for reading,

> Parents play roles of inestimable importance in laying the foundation for learning to read. A parent is a child's first guide through a vast and unfamiliar world. A parent is a child's first mentor on what words mean and how to mean things with words. A parent is a child's first tutor in unraveling the fascinating puzzle of written language. A parent is a child's one enduring source of faith that somehow, sooner or later, he or she will become a good reader. (p. 28)

Becoming a Nation of Readers concludes with a statement that is at the heart of *Ready for Reading,* "On a more sober note, parents' good intentions for their children are not enough. Parents must put their intentions into practice if their children are to have the foundation required for success in reading" (p. 28).

What does the home that sends children to school ready to read look like? It often has the following characteristics:

❖ *It is a home where children see their parents reading regularly and obviously valuing and enjoying the process.*

One of our concerns when we began to write this book was that we would give the impression that reading to children must always be a formal learning experience. We cannot state too strongly that this is not the case.

Mary Renck Jalongo (1988) tells us that the process of learning to read must *begin* with enjoyment. Pleasure persuades the child first to look, then to discuss and listen, next to remember, and finally to read a favorite book. Enjoyment, says Jalongo, is the force that sustains a young child's involvement when toys and television beckon. We hope that children come to view reading good literature as something fun. We want them to see reading as an enjoyable, positive way to spend their time. It is best when this happens naturally, as when children see powerful role models consistently engaged in, and enjoying, the reading process. These role models can be brothers or sisters, aunts or uncles, grandparents, and, most importantly, parents.

When children are in home environments where they see Dad reading a magazine, Mom reading the newspaper, and Grandma reading a novel, they become very comfortable with the idea that reading is important. Better yet, when Dad says to Mom, "This magazine has the greatest information on how to make our computer more efficient," and Mom replies, "I just read something about that in the paper," and Grandma states, "Please be quiet, I'm at a really good part," children know that reading can be informative and enjoyable. Finally, when a parent says to a child, "Why don't you go get one of your books and join us?" that parent is inviting his or her child to become a member of the reading community. In this environment, the chances are excellent that the child will join and become a lifelong member. Important research by Kenneth Rowe (1991) demonstrated that the strongest predictors of reading success for fifth graders were reading independently and talking about books with family and friends.

❖ *It is a home rich in literature.*

Newspapers, magazines, novels, and children's books are found in abundance in the home rich in literature. This is a home where children have their own bookcases in their bedrooms. In the previous section, we talked about the importance of children being in an environment where they see good role models (parents, grandparents, brothers and sisters, and others) appreciating and enjoying the reading process. This environment becomes even richer when literature of all kinds is seen by the child as a very natural part of the home. Magazines, coffee table books, newspapers, recipes, books of all shapes and sizes, and bookcases all are experienced by the child to be as much a part of the home as tables and chairs and lamps and sofas. Any home with children is likely to have a refrigerator groaning under the load of pictures, cartoons, and student work and accomplishments attached to the exterior. The home rich in literature very often goes a step further and has newspaper clippings, humorous poems, and inspirational sayings. It is not unusual to find kids clustered around the refrigerator, not for food, but for entertainment and information!

In addition to books of all shapes and sizes, there should be books from a wide variety of genres. It is a home truly rich in literature when fiction is found alongside nonfiction, and poetry is next to picture books. Folktales, fables, myths, and science fiction can be found. It is also important that a child's own books be varied. Later in this book, we will discuss the importance of alphabet books, books that play with sounds, children's books of poetry, nonfiction books, predictable books, and books that deal with important moments in children's lives. Each of these should have a central place in the home.

❖ *It is a home where the local library is a familiar and important place.*

The library is much more than a place filled with books. Libraries house the thinking of individuals who have shaped the way society works. Children who understand what libraries are about and how libraries work have the knowledge of the world at their fingertips! Anything they want to know lies waiting to be discovered in a good library. Yet, there are children who can program a VCR, tame the most complex microwave oven, and make video games dance at their command who are ignorant about how to check out a book from the library. Parents should ask themselves some important questions: "Have I been to the toy store with my children more often than I have been with them to the library?" "Can my children find and check out a video from the video store yet not do the same with a book from the library?" The family that visits the library weekly, with each member of the family checking out a variety of books, very naturally produces children who become friends with the library. When a father and child walk through the library to find a book on how to raise their new puppy, then head to the children's section to find *Clifford, the Big Red Dog* (Bridwell, 1988), then walk together to the checkout counter, each using his or her own library card to check out books, the library becomes a friendly and useful environment.

❖ *It is a home where children are read to regularly.*

Almost universal agreement exists that the single most important factor in developing the background necessary for success in reading is for children to have been read to aloud. Reading aloud regularly to children in their early years is critical to their later reading achievement (Spear-Swerling & Sternberg, 1996). It is not just reading to children, however, that is important. Equally important is the way books are read and the discussions parents have with their children as they read. Questions such as "What would you do if you were Curious George?", which prompt children to think about ideas in a book, are important in literacy development and are not unlike questions teachers will ask in school. When children encounter these questions at home, they are often much more comfortable and successful with teachers' questions. Conversations about the meanings of less familiar words also support literacy development. For example, when you read about a fleet of ships that arrives in the harbor in *The Man Who Loved Books* by Jean Fritz, take a moment to discuss the meaning of the word *fleet.*

As children are read to regularly, they also gain knowledge of how books work. They know where books begin and where they end; they recognize that people (who read English) read from left to right and from top to bottom. Most significantly, they learn that books have important and enjoyable things to say to them. A child who enters school knowing how "to turn a book on" is a child who will find learning to read a much gentler and more successful endeavor.

As children are read to regularly, they develop an "ear" for the language of literature. They become comfortable with the way written words are put together and the way sentences and stories are supposed to sound. When children hear Bill Martin, Jr.'s (1996) "Brown Bear, Brown Bear, What do you see? I see a redbird looking at me. Redbird, redbird, What do you see? I see a yellow duck looking at me" or Bill Martin, Jr. and John Archambault's (1989) "**A** told **B**, and **B** told **C**, 'I'll meet you at the top of the coconut tree.' 'Whee!' said **D** to **E F G**, 'I'll beat you to the top of the coconut tree,'" they are discovering the predictability of written words. When this happens, learning to read is often a much easier process.

Finally, and probably most importantly, children who are read to regularly associate reading with a time of warmth and closeness with their parents. These children enter school with a tremendous advantage. Reading is viewed as a positive part of their lives, as something they want to do.

❖ *It is a home where parents provide encouragement and motivation.*

The five characteristics discussed above will often produce children who enter school ready to read. However, it is the home where parents, on a consistent basis, encourage their children to involve themselves in reading- and writing-related activities that most often develops children who will be successful in school. In fact, homes that encourage reading and writing by having paper, pencil, crayon, chalk, and even chalkboards readily available to children are developing characteristics in children that will allow them to enter school with confidence. Reading researcher Dolores Durkin (1966) labeled children from these homes "paper and pencil kids." She found that it was not intelligence or social class that produced kids who enter school already reading. She discovered that successful readers came from homes where someone read to them, someone answered their questions, and the children liked to write or make marks on paper. Many children write *before* they begin reading. Parents who encourage their children to experiment with writing often are helping them ease into reading. However, these parents do not expect perfect handwriting, spelling, or grammar. They are very accepting of their child's attempts to write.

One of the best, and most natural, forms of motivation is when parents present children with books that focus on important moments in their lives. By sharing books at times such as those in the following list, children see that books have significant things to say about issues that are very important to them. They see a reason for reading, a reason for books.

A New Puppy. When a child gets a new puppy, he or she should receive right along with it any of Norman Bridwell's *Clifford, The Big Red Dog* books or Marc Brown's *Arthur's New Puppy. Puppy Care and Critters, Too!* by Judy Petersen-Fleming and Bill Fleming presents information on pet care that any new young owner will appreciate, and *My Puppy Is Born* by Joanna Cole helps children understand the birth and development process of a young puppy.

An Important Excursion. When a trip to the zoo is planned, providing children with books such as Eric Carle's *1, 2, 3 to the Zoo*, Christopher Maynard's *Amazing Animal Babies*, or Ivan Chermayeff's *Furry Facts* is an important part of the preparation. When a trip to the beach is planned, reading *Seashore* by Donald Silver, *Tide Pool* by Christiane Gunzi, and *Henry and Mudge and the Forever Sea* by Cynthia Rylant can enhance the experience.

The Birth of a Sibling. When a sibling is born, *Welcoming Babies* by Margy Burns Knight can be shared to introduce children to a variety of cultural traditions for celebrating the arrival of infants.

Time with Mom or Dad. When a child is set to go on a special outing with his or her dad, reading together Mercer Mayer's *Just Me and My Dad* is a must.

A Loose Tooth. Little is more important to a child than that first loose tooth. This is a perfect time to read Lucy Bate's *Little Rabbit's Loose Tooth* or Marc Brown's *Arthur's Tooth.*

A Nightmare. When literature can help a child cope with nightmares, then books become important indeed. Mercer Mayer's *There's a Nightmare in My Closet* helps children deal with nightmares.

The First Athletic Event. This can be an anxiety-producing time. *Ronald Morgan Goes to Bat* by Patricia Reilly Giff helps reduce the anxiety.

The Hospital. Curious George Goes to the Hospital by Margaret and H. A. Rey helps make a hospital stay a much more manageable occasion.

A Rainy Day. Rainy days can become a time of enchantment when *Cloudy with a Chance of Meatballs* by Judi Barrett and *The Napping House* by Audrey Wood are read. In fact, every time it rains chances are that one or the other (or both!) of these two books will be placed in a parent's hands to be read. *A Rainy Day* by Sandra Markle offers scientific information about rain, which may be shared as parents and child explore their wet world.

Death of a Pet. This can be a very traumatic time for a young child. *The Tenth Good Thing about Barney* by Judith Viorst is a fine book for helping children work through this difficult period.

The process of reading to children wonderful literature that deals with significant issues and events in their lives is a powerful way to encourage them to turn to good books for information, comfort, and entertainment. Children who are read to become adults who clearly recognize the value of literature.

Motivation is every bit as important as encouragement in producing successful readers. Parents who tell their preschoolers how enjoyable school can be, all that can be learned there, and how well they know their children will do are doing much to send their children to school in the frame of mind that school is something to be eagerly anticipated. However, parents who, intentionally or unintentionally, give their children the impression that reading and school were "really tough back then" and will be "even tougher for you kids today" are creating very negative concepts in very impressionable young minds. The research suggests that children who have success in school and in reading most often have parents who highly value education and reading (Downing, 1987) and express these values to their children. For many of these parents, having children who do not learn to read and come to know the joy of a good book is unthinkable!

Involving preschoolers in literacy activities is essential to producing students ready to read. This is demonstrated in the research of Gordon Wells (1986). Wells started looking at 132 children just after their first birthday. He actually attached small microphones to their clothing that automatically came on at different intervals during each day. In this way, Wells was able to hear how many "literacy events" the children were engaged in. Wells found that one child had been involved in over 6,000 literacy events before beginning school. He found another child who was not read to once before starting school. When the children in Wells's study were given school entrance assessments, the child who had participated in over 6,000 literacy events ranked at the top while the child with no experiences ranked at the bottom. A predictable but unfortunate finding of Wells's research was that when the students were evaluated at the end of the elementary years, the ranking of these two children had not changed. All those years of schooling were probably not as important to student success as a home rich in literacy activities.

In summary, let us examine a "baker's dozen" benefits children gain from participating in literature activities with their parents:

1. They learn how books work.
2. They come to know the "language of literature."
3. They see that books have important things to say to them.
4. They develop positive attitudes toward reading.

5. They develop the desire to read.

6. They expand their literary interests.

7. They expand their vocabulary.

8. Their ability to understand what is being read improves.

9. They learn how libraries work.

10. They see connections between reading and writing.

11. They significantly increase their chances for success in school.

12. They come to view reading as an important part of their lives.

13. They know an abundance of wonderful literature is available to them.

Based on the information presented in this chapter, it seems appropriate to conclude that not only are parents their children's first teachers but also they are their children's most important teachers. If this is the case, then, parents need to have a clear understanding of what reading and the skills of reading are. Chapter Two will address these important issues.

References

Allington, R., & Walmsley, S. (1995). No quick fix: Where do we go from here? In R. Allington & S. Walmsley (Eds.), *No Quick Fix: Rethinking Literacy Programs in America's Elementary Schools.* New York: Teachers College Press.

Becoming a Nation of Readers. (1985). Washington, DC: The National Institute of Education.

Celebrating the National Reading Initiative. (1989). Sacramento: California State Department of Education.

Downing, J. (1987). Comparative perspectives on world literacy. In D. A. Wagner (Ed.), *The Future of Literacy in a Changing World.* New York: Pergamon.

Durkin, D. (1966). *Children Who Read Early.* New York: Teachers College Press.

Huck, C. S., Hepler, S., & Hickman, J. (1987). *Children's Literature in the Elementary School.* New York: Holt, Rinehart & Winston.

Jalongo, M. R. (1988). *Young Children and Picture Books.* Washington, DC: National Association for the Education of Young Children.

Rowe, K. J. (1991). The influence of reading activity at home on students' attitudes towards reading, classroom attentiveness and reading achievement: An application of structural equation modeling. *British Journal of Educational Psychology, 61,* 19–35.

Snow, C. E., Burns, M. S., & Griffin, P. (Eds.) (1998). *Preventing Reading Difficulties in Young Children.* Washington, DC: National Academy Press.

Spear-Swerling, L., & Sternberg, R. (1996). *Off Track: When Poor Readers Become "Learning Disabled."* Boulder, CO: Westview Press.

Stanovich, K. E. (1993–94). Romance and reality. *The Reading Teacher, 47,* 280–291.

Stanovich, K. E. (1986). Matthew effects in reading: Some consequences of individual differences in the acquisition of literacy. *Reading Research Quarterly, 21,* 360–407.

Wells, G. (1986). *The Meaning Makers: Children Learning Language and Using Language to Learn.* Portsmouth, NH: Heinemann.

Children's Books Cited

Barrett, J. (1985). *Cloudy with a Chance of Meatballs.* New York: Live Oak Media.

Bate, L. (1983). *Little Rabbit's Loose Tooth.* New York: Crown.

Bridwell, N. (1988). *Clifford, the Big Red Dog.* New York: Scholastic.

Brown, M. (1995). *Arthur's New Puppy.* Boston: Little Brown.

Brown, M. (1985). *Arthur's Tooth.* New York: Trumpet.

Carle, E. (1996). *1, 2, 3 to the Zoo.* New York: Philomel.

Chermayeff, I. (1994). *Furry Facts.* San Diego, CA: Harcourt Brace.

Cole, J. (1991). *My Puppy is Born.* New York: William Morrow.

Fritz, J. (1981). *The Man Who Loved Books.* New York: G. P. Putnam's Sons.

Giff, P. R. (1990). *Ronald Morgan Goes to Bat.* New York: Viking.

Gunzi, C. (1998). *Tide Pool.* La Vergne, TN: DK Publishing.

Knight, M. B. (1994). *Welcoming Babies.* Gardiner, ME: Tilbury House.

Markle, S. (1993). *A Rainy Day.* New York: Orchard.

Martin, B., Jr. (1996). *Brown Bear, Brown Bear, What Do You See?* New York: Holt.

Martin, B., Jr., & Archambault, J. (1989). *Chicka Chicka Boom Boom.* New York: Scholastic.

Mayer, M. (1982). *Just Me and My Dad.* New York: Golden.

Mayer, M. (1992). *There's a Nightmare in My Closet.* New York: E. P. Dutton.

Maynard, C. (1993). *Amazing Animal Babies.* New York: Alfred A. Knopf.

Petersen-Fleming, J., & Fleming, B. (1994). *Puppy Care and Critters, Too!* New York: William Morrow.

Rey, M., & Rey, H. A. (1976). *Curious George Goes to the Hospital.* Boston: Houghton Mifflin.

Rylant, C. (1989). *Henry and Mudge and the Forever Sea.* New York: Scholastic.

Silver, D. M. (1997). *Seashore.* New York: McGraw-Hill.

Viorst, J. (1971). *The Tenth Good Thing about Barney.* New York: Atheneum.

Wood, A. (1983). *The Napping House.* San Diego, CA: Harcourt Brace Jovanovich.

Chapter Two

What Is Reading?

*L*et us begin our examination of reading by looking at dictionary definitions.

- ✦ The word *read* is defined in *Webster's New World Dictionary and Thesaurus* (1996) as "to get the meaning of writing by interpreting the characters."

- ✦ It is defined in the *Oxford American Dictionary* (1980) as "to be able to understand the meaning of written or printed words or symbols."

- ✦ In *Merriam Webster's Collegiate Dictionary* (1996), the word *read* is defined as "to receive or take in the sense of as letters or symbols especially by sight or touch."

Notice that each of these definitions makes reference to symbols or characters and to meaning. Understanding how we use the symbols of written language and how we make meaning from text is essential to our understanding of reading. In this chapter, we will discuss these two aspects of reading.

Reading Is a Decoding Process

Reading is a complex process that involves dealing with the symbol system of written language. In English, this means understanding that the symbols we call *letters* represent the sounds of our language and that these sounds combine to make words, which represent ideas. Understanding this system and being able to use this understanding to figure out printed words is what educators refer to as *decoding*.

It is, without a doubt, critical that children learn the symbol, or code, system of their written language. They need to be able to use this code system to access the thoughts and ideas of others; they need to be able to use it for expressing their own thoughts and ideas in writing.

Centuries ago, human beings began recording their ideas in written form. This form differed around the world, and today a tremendous variety of written language systems exists. In order for people in a culture to communicate with one another using written symbols, they must understand the system their culture uses for recording ideas. Figuring out what the written code is—what the symbols represent—is crucial to being able to read.

Teachers know there are a number of ways to help children figure out the written code of the English language. We provide a brief summary of several decoding strategies.

Phonics

Many people have heard the term *phonics*. In fact, it is often the subject of some debate. It refers to the attaching of a sound to a symbol or group of symbols. The printed letter *"p,"* for example, represents the sound heard at the beginning of the word *popcorn* and the end of *top*. When *"c"* and *"h"* are combined (*"ch"*), they represent the sound heard at the beginning of *chicken* and the end of *much*. If children know the sounds that are represented by the letters in words, they may use this knowledge to identify words, such as the following:

    cat
    fish
    jump

Structural Analysis

To figure out some words, it is helpful to look at the parts of the words: prefixes (as in the underlined parts of <u>re</u>play, <u>sub</u>terranean, and <u>inter</u>action), suffixes (kind<u>ness</u>, suggest<u>able</u>), inflectional endings (start<u>ed</u>, swift<u>ly</u>), and root words (un<u>comfort</u>able, dis<u>advantage</u>). What can appear to be an overwhelming task of decoding a long word can be made simpler by looking for familiar pieces. Older children, for example, can decode the word *unforgettable* by peeling off the prefix "un" and the suffix "able." What remains is the word *forget[t]*. Once the root word *forget* is decoded, the reader can reattach the prefix and suffix to decode the entire word. See if you can use structural analysis to decode the following words.

unambiguously
intergenerational
departmentalizing

If these examples are words you hear or use in speech, once you decode them you can turn your attention to their meaning and keep reading. If you are unfamiliar with the words, then you may be able to use your knowledge of the parts of the words to make sense of them.

Analogies

Children learn to decode some words by comparing them to words they already know. For example, if they encounter the word *rat*, they might think of the known word *cat* and figure out the word by analogy. If they come across the word *lump*, they might think of the word *jump*. The known word will help them identify the unknown word.

Sight Words

Some children enter school already knowing a number of words by sight. That is, they know immediately what a word is when they see it. These words are typically ones that hold great significance for children, such as their own names or the names of family members, including *Mommy* and *Daddy*. Some children recognize the words *dog* and *cat*. Other words, if seen in context, also may be part of a child's sight word storehouse. *STOP*, when seen on a red sign on a street corner, is easily read by many children. Brand names of familiar products often become sight words. How do children learn these words? By exposure to them multiple times.

Some words in written English must be learned by sight. They are words that phonics, structural analysis, and analogy cannot help us to figure out. Think about the words listed next. Can you sound them out? Does looking at word parts help? Can you think of other words almost like them and use your knowledge of those words to figure out these words? No. These are words we simply must memorize.

of
island
suite
once
said

Context Clues

Context clues include the information we get from a sentence or passage that help us figure out a word. For example, if you do not know the last word in the sentence below (presented as "xxx"), you can use information from the rest of the sentence and your knowledge of the world to make a likely prediction. Try reading the sentence.

My car ran out of xxx.

What did you say? Gas? Oil? Water? Why? Because these words make sense in the context of the rest of the sentence. The five words preceding "xxx" helped you with "xxx." You made a reasonable guess because you know something about cars and what they might run out of. You have possibly even had the experience of running out of gas (or oil or water). Proceeding in your reading may yield additional information that will narrow the logical choices. Your knowledge of language also assisted you in your efforts to figure out the word. You know what makes sense grammatically; that is, you know that your unknown word is not a verb (even if you cannot define "verb")—you would not have said, "My car ran out of <u>swim</u>" or "My car ran out of <u>ski</u>." And you know that your unknown word is not an adjective—you would not have said, "My car ran out of <u>pretty</u>" or "My car ran out of <u>blue</u>." Nor is the unknown word a preposition—you would not have said, "My car ran out of <u>with</u>" or "My car ran out of <u>from</u>." Only a noun would work in this position in this sentence.

Now try decoding the underlined word in the sentence pairs below:

The girl tied the <u>bow</u> on her dress.

The girl took a <u>bow</u> at the end of the performance.

"<u>Wind</u>!" the frustrated woman shouted into the air, "Stop blowing my papers away!"

"<u>Wind</u>!" she suggested. "Try winding the watch before you throw it away!"

Context provides the reader with important information. In the case of these sentences, the only way that we are able to determine how to pronounce "bow" and "wind" is by the context in which the word appears.

You only can use context, however, if you are reading for meaning. If you are simply saying the words, then context will not help you decode unknown words. This, then, leads us to the other (and more important) part of reading: Reading is a meaning-making process.

Reading Is a Meaning-Making Process

As the definitions at the beginning of this chapter indicate, decoding is not all there is to reading. It is not enough just to say the words. You must make sense of them. Just because you can say the words on a page does not mean that you have *read* the page. Consider the following two sets of examples.

The first set is written in languages other than English. Try saying the following sentences:

> Tengo un gato bonito.   (Spanish)
> Medizin ist in ein Flasche.   (German)
> Kumusta ka?   (Tagalog)
> Je suis perdu.   (French)
> Tutti i bambini sono carini.   (Italian)

Possibly, you said the sentences reasonably well; that is, you gave a fairly accurate representation of them in speech. You decoded them. However, unless you are a speaker of these languages, you have no idea what they mean.

Next is a set of examples provided in English. Test your understanding of the following:

> When England's pride is at stake, few take it more to heart than Jon Baynard. Last week in Harare, he was the stroke player on rations, defying an ebullient Zimbabwe attack in excess of seven hours, to score an unbeaten century, his tenth at test level. England now leads by a wide margin.

> "Are you in?"
> "Sure!" shouted the girl. "But no babes, and rainbows are in."
> "Okay. Limbo!" The young girl ran to the wall and hoped to be called first.

> Keep the tapered surface flat on the bed of the joiner.

> Tiny edge stitches on the piped neckline and shoulder seams, a blind front placket, and knotted buttons produce simple elegance.

> The notes were sour because the seam split.

Again, you probably were able to orally reproduce the passages, but it is unlikely that you understood all of them. And, had you been required to read them for some important purpose, it would have been a frustrating experience for you. Good readers expect that print will make sense; otherwise, what is the point of reading?

Reading is a thinking process in which the reader makes meaning from the print. All parents hope that their children can say the words on a page, but few of us would be satisfied if this was all our children could do. In fact, we would be very concerned if our children were not able to understand what they were reading.

The expectation that text carries meaning is so important that we must be conscientious about nurturing it in our children. As you read aloud to your child, you expose him or her to the fact that books contain ideas, whether those books are make-believe stories or informational texts about real people, places, and things, that books are enjoyable, and that they are relevant. As you sit close to your child and share a book with him or her—as you talk about and respond to the book—your child comes to understand that words on the page represent meaning. You laugh together at a character's predicament, such as when The Hungry Thing, in the book of the same name by Jan Slepian and Ann Seidler, cannot get the townspeople to understand what he wants to eat. You compare a shell you found on the beach to pictures in *Starfish, Seashells, and Crabs* by George Fichter. You race outside to make angels in the snow after reading *The Snowy Day* by Ezra Jack Keats. As you share a book with your child, you provide your child with the expectation that an author's words will make sense and be interesting. You lay the foundation for your child's future interactions with books—a foundation that is critical to reading—the idea that books communicate a message and are sources of entertainment and information.

As any parent knows, children ask a lot of questions. What a thrill it is when a young child turns to a book to look for answers. One of the authors' sons, Billy, was given a model dinosaur when he was seven years old. Curious about what kind of dinosaur it was, he trotted down the hall and returned with a book. Flopping down on the floor beside his mother, he turned the pages until he found a picture of a dinosaur that looked like his model. He joyfully shared his discovery, and then, perusing the rest of the book, asked questions that were sparked by other pictures in the book. Mother and son shared the book together, both learning some interesting facts about dinosaurs.

Another one of our children, Peter, recently decided that he wanted to build a bird house. When he and his father started developing plans, Peter suddenly stopped, said, "Wait a minute, Dad," then ran from the garage into the house. He hunted through three bookcases before he found what he wanted: *I Can't Wait Until Christmas* by Linda Lee Maifair. Why this book? Because in it Big Bird (of Sesame Street fame) builds a bird house for his grandmother as a Christmas gift. Peter wanted to use the pictures in the book as a model for his own bird house.

Five-year-old Danny just discovered his first loose tooth. He played with it with his tongue all day, talked about it over dinner, and called his cousins to share his excitement. At bedtime, Danny pulled books from the shelves in his

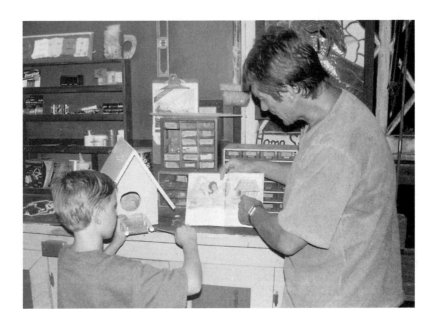

room for his parents to read. What did they discover at the top of the stack? *Arthur's Tooth* by Marc Brown.

What is it that made these children turn to books at these moments? It was their many previous experiences with books. Each of them had learned long ago that books are wonderful resources, full of fascinating information about the world. And, each had learned that books have personal value. Books address issues we care about.

The ability to make meaning as we read is dependent on a number of things. The first, as we have stated, is our understanding that this is the purpose of reading. Other factors that strongly influence a reader's ability to make meaning are the reader's background knowledge, language, and active participation in the act of reading.

❖ *Meaning making is influenced by the reader's background knowledge.*

Much research of the past few decades has demonstrated that good readers bring their knowledge of the world and their background of experiences to the printed page, *and* that their knowledge and experiences greatly influence whether or not, and how well, they understand a passage. Reading researchers Linda Fielding and P. David Pearson summarize this research by saying that comprehension "depends heavily on knowledge" (1994, p. 62).

The examples written in English at the beginning of this chapter illustrate this point. Unless you have relevant expertise or background knowledge about the topics of the passages and were able to call to mind that knowledge, chances are the passages did not hold meaning for you. Thus, you did not truly *read* the passages. Reading requires understanding. Let us look at the examples again.

> When England's pride is at stake, few take it more to heart than Jon Baynard. Last week in Harare, he was the stroke player on rations, defying an ebullient Zimbabwe attack in excess of seven hours, to score an unbeaten century, his tenth at test level. England now leads by a wide margin.

> "Are you in?"
> "Sure!" shouted the girl. "But no babes, and rainbows are in."
> "Okay. Limbo!" The young girl ran to the wall and hoped to be called first.

> Keep the tapered surface flat on the bed of the joiner.

> Tiny edge stitches on the piped neckline and shoulder seams, a blind front placket, and knotted buttons produce simple elegance.

> The notes were sour because the seam split.

The first passage is about a game of cricket, the second passage is about a children's handball game, the topics of the third and fourth are woodworking and sewing, respectively, and the fifth is about bagpipes. You may or may not possess sufficient background knowledge to make meaning from the first four passages, but you probably are able to make sense of the fifth only once you learn it is about bagpipes. When the seam on a bagpipe splits, the notes are no longer on pitch. (The sentence appeared in a research study conducted by John Bransford and N. McCarrell in 1974.) Reading requires that we have and use our knowledge of the world in order to make sense of printed language.

Because no text is completely self-explanatory, good readers constantly use their own knowledge to fill in the gaps and make sense of what is written. Think about the following passage:

> The boy walked up to the librarian and handed her his card. She smiled at him as she took the items he set on her desk and, one by one, slid them into the machine. When she handed them back to him, along with his card, he said, "See you next month!" and walked down the hallway and out the door.

What information did you bring to this text in order to understand it? If you have had experiences with libraries, you probably made the following inferences: the card was a library card (not a birthday card); the items were probably, but not necessarily, books (not fast food items); the boy said, "See you next month" because the items are due in a month. Furthermore, the boy may be a regular visitor or he would just return the items to an outside bin. You made sense of the passage by using your knowledge of the world. Also, you expected the passage to make sense, and so you were actively involved in thinking about its meaning as you read it.

Because background knowledge plays a powerful role in understanding text, an individual with many library experiences understands a passage about libraries with much greater ease than a person with no or limited experiences (real or vicarious) with a library. Golfers can read golf magazines with greater understanding than individuals who do not golf or follow the sport, even if nongolfers can pronounce each word in the magazine with ease. Doctors read medical journals with greater understanding than highly educated professionals in other fields (who, in turn, read research in their own areas of expertise with greater understanding than doctors who have limited background in these other fields). Those with considerable expertise in computers read computer magazines, even ads about computers in the newspaper or popular magazines, with greater comprehension than many of us because they work with and think about computers frequently. They know the jargon; they know how one idea follows or fits with the next. They can fill in the gaps.

Some people do not have enough knowledge of a topic to understand a passage; many of us feel this way about interpreting certain legal documents or income tax manuals or even directions on setting up a new VCR. Other people have the knowledge, but may not make use of it during reading. This may have been the case for you with the bagpipe example. As parents, we want both to build background knowledge by providing many experiences for our children and to encourage them to use their knowledge during reading by helping them make connections between what they hear during a read-aloud experience and what they know.

One final example of the role of background knowledge in reading: Have you ever read a book at one age, then read it again at another age and responded differently to the second reading? The book did not change over time—you did. Your experiences were different, your background knowledge was different—so your understanding of the book was different.

❖ *Meaning making is influenced by the reader's language development.*

What we read is *language* in written form. The words we use to communicate in speech have been put in writing. Typically, however, written language is more formal than spoken language. Even some books for very young children use quite complex sentence structure and sophisticated words. This sentence from *Winnie the Pooh's Halloween* by Bruce Talkington illustrates this point well.

> *The late afternoon sun appeared to hesitate on the horizon, settling comfortably among the tip-top branches of the trees of the Hundred-Acre Wood as if reluctant to turn off its light and make way for the night.*

If children have not heard this kind of complex language in read-aloud experiences, they will have more difficulty understanding what they are reading when they encounter these sentences later.

The more developed children's language, the more likely they will make sense of what they read. The richer their oral language and the more they experience the language of books, the more likely they are to make sense of written language. The broader their vocabulary and the more sophisticated their sentence structure, the more likely they are to make sense of what they see in print.

Research has shown that an effective way to broaden a child's vocabulary is through reading. We also know that children's syntax (the way in which words are put together to form phrases, clauses, or sentences) is a reflection of the language they have been exposed to. If you speak in short sentences to your child, often your child will speak in short sentences. If you use more complex language (as long as it is understandable), your child is more likely to use and be comfortable with complex language. Books are a wonderful source of more complex language structures.

Think about the type of language that children are exposed to through their experiences with books.

Complex Sentence Structure

Brother and Sister Bear, who lived with their mama and papa in the big tree house down a sunny dirt road deep in Bear country, looked quite a lot alike.

   —*The Berenstain Bears Learn About Strangers* by Stan and Jan Berenstain

Late that evening, when all the shoppers had gone and the doors were shut and locked, Corduroy climbed carefully down from his shelf and began searching everywhere on the floor for his lost button.

   —*Corduroy* by Don Freeman

Off they went, scampering across fields while avoiding the cows and down a dirt lane, edged with bright flowers, until at last they reached the cobblestones leading into town.

   —*The Town Mouse and the Country Mouse* by Lorinda Bryan Cauley

Language Unique to Stories

Once upon a time . . .

. . . and they lived happily ever after.

Back in the rugged pioneer days . . .
> —*Pecos Bill* by Steven Kellogg

Mature Linguistic Expressions

As they drew near, the bear stood up and politely raised its hat.
> —*Paddington Bear* by Michael Bond

She grew more and more frightened.
> —*Rumpelstiltskin* by Paul O. Zelinsky

Hermit Crab was forever growing too big for the house on his back.
> —*Is This a House for Hermit Crab?* by Megan McDonald

But their mother was greatly displeased.
> —*The Poky Little Puppy* by Janette Sebring Lowrey

This creature is an OCTOPUS and very often hides by changing to the color . . . over which it glides.
> —*How to Hide an Octopus* by Ruth Heller

Vocabulary

Her stepmother, the Queen, was cruel and vain. She hated anyone whose beauty rivaled her own—and she watched her stepdaughter with angry, jealous eyes.
> —*Walt Disney's Snow White and the Seven Dwarfs* by Rita Balducci

The second day the queen had inquiries made in town, searching for new names.
> —*Rumpelstiltskin* by Paul O. Zelinsky

Six sleepy sheep slumbered on six soft pillows in one big bed . . .
> —*Six Sleepy Sheep* by Jeffie Ross Gordon

In a warm and sultry forest far, far away . . .
> —*Stellaluna* by Janell Cannon

Parents' verbal interactions with their children support language growth which, as we know, is important for reading. Particularly important is the use

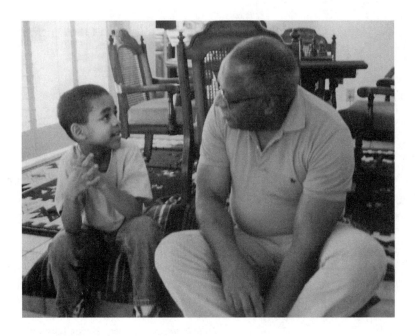

of what is called "decontextualized language." Simply put, decontextualized language refers to conversations or discussions about nonimmediate topics. To fully understand this concept, we first need to examine examples of immediate or contextualized language:

"Put that down!"

"Do you need to use the rest room before we go?"

"Let's get in the car now."

"Time to eat!"

Each of these statements addresses something that is relevant in the children's lives at the moment it is said. It is talk about the here and now.

In contrast, the following are some examples of decontextualized language:

"I wonder how your friend felt when he fell off his bike."

"Remember last year when we went to the mountains?"

"What do you think we should do for your cousin's birthday?"

"Do you know what I read about crocodiles today? They are . . . "

Decontextualized language asks children to think beyond the here and now. Familiarity with decontextualized language helps prepare children for school-related activities and learnings. Books are one excellent source of decontextualized language.

Background knowledge and language are powerful players in making meaning. But there is more. We turn to a third aspect next.

❖ *Meaning making is influenced by active engagement with the text.*

Good readers think about what they read. They anticipate what is coming; they react to what happens; they make connections between what they read and what they have experienced; they create images of characters, settings, and situations. Have you ever read a book and then later seen a movie made from the book? Did you think, "I didn't picture it like that," or "Meryl Streep would have fit that part better"? These feelings reveal that you were an active reader—you created images in your mind when you read the book. Unfortunately, these images did not agree with the movie maker's images!

Involvement with a text is important in reading. How do you know that your child is involved with a read-aloud book? Usually you can tell by his or her verbal responses. Does your child ask questions in the middle of the book? "Who is that guy?" "Why did he do that?" Does he or she predict what is going to happen next? "Oh, no! I'll bet they find him hiding in the dog house!" Does he or she laugh aloud or respond in other ways to what has happened?

One way to encourage active participation is to select books that are personally meaningful. If your child is fascinated by cars, read books about cars. If your child is anticipating the arrival of a younger sibling, read books about new additions to families. Children will listen, ask questions, talk about related experiences, and offer their own points of view.

Another way to encourage engagement is to read what are known as "predictable" books. Predictable books are those with which, by virtue of the book's pattern, children can successfully anticipate the next word or next sentence. Their predictability encourages participation and engages children's minds. Often, these books make heavy use of rhyme or repetition. In many books, pictures provide excellent clues about the print. Additional techniques authors use in writing predictable books include the following:

◆ *Cumulative Patterns.* *The Napping House* (Wood, 1983) follows a cumulative pattern. So do many other children's books, such as *Hairy Maclarey from Donaldson's Dairy* (Dodd, 1983), *The House That Jack Built* (Falconer, 1994), *I Know an Old Lady Who Swallowed a Fly* (Westcott, 1988), and *The*

Gingerbread Boy (Galdone, 1983). In each of these stories, what happened before is repeated. The book starts with a phrase or sentence, adding another on each successive page, repeating the sentences from previous pages. For example:

This is the house that Jack built.

This is the malt
That lay in the house that Jack built.

This is the rat
That ate the malt
That lay in the house that Jack built.

And so on.

✦ *Repetition.* When phrases are repeated several times within a book, children quickly notice the repetition, come to anticipate it, and can join in the story. In *The Three Little Pigs and the Big Bad Wolf* (Rounds, 1992), the wolf knocks on each pig's door, shouting, "Little pig! Little pig! Let me come in!" The pigs respond, "No! No! By the hairs on my chinny-chin-chin, I'll not let you in." The wolf says, "Then I'll huff and I'll puff and I'll blow your house in!" In *The Little Red Hen* (Galdone, 1985), the animals repeat, "Not I" each time the hen asks for their help. Few children can resist joining in each time their parents read these sections in the stories.

Brown Bear, Brown Bear, What Do You See? (Martin, 1996) and *Polar Bear, Polar Bear, What Do You Hear?* (Martin, 1997) are highly predictable books that use repetition, rhyme, and rhythm.

✦ *Rhyme and Rhythm.* Some books make use of rhyme and rhythm. The chanting nature of these books, along with the rhyming scheme, makes them predictable. In the passage "Sipping once, sipping twice, sipping chicken soup with _____," you likely want to say "rice." You probably will not say "vegetables" or "noodles" even though these choices make sense. "Rice" fits because it rhymes with "twice" and because it follows the rhythmical pattern. Sendak's (1962) *Chicken Soup with Rice* is one of many books that uses rhyme and rhythm.

✦ *Sequential Patterns.* Books that follow a familiar sequence, such as letters of the alphabet, days of the week, or the numbers 1 to 10 also prompt participation. *The Very Hungry Caterpillar* (Carle, 1986) uses numbers and days of the week as a caterpillar eats through a variety of foods.

✦ *Interlocking Patterns.* Some books follow a pattern in which the pieces interconnect so much that each piece depends on the preceding piece. For example, in *If You Give a Mouse a Cookie* (Numeroff, 1985), the mouse gets a cookie. Because he has a cookie, he becomes thirsty and wants a glass of milk. Once he gets the milk, he needs a straw, and so on.

We suggest many predictable books in Part II of this book.

Books that require physical manipulation, such as lifting a flap, pulling a tab, or sliding a panel, also invite active participation. Eric Hill's *Spot* books, such as *Spot Goes to the Beach* and *Spot Goes to the Farm,* are wonderful examples of this technique as are Stephen Savage's *Animals under Cover* and Charles Reasoner's *Who's in the Sea?*

When we read aloud to young children, we should help the children engage in meaningful ways with the texts. Some researchers are discovering that children whom are read to aloud with an interactive style have a greater understanding of the text than children whose parents or teachers read aloud without encouraging the children to interact with the text. Noted educational researcher Marilyn Adams states,

> It is not just reading to children that makes the difference, it is enjoying the books with them and reflecting on their form and content. It is developing and supporting the children's curiosity about text and the meanings it conveys. It is encouraging the children to examine the print. It is sometimes starting and always inviting discussions of the meanings of the words and the relationships of the text's ideas to the world beyond the book. And it is showing the children that we value and enjoy reading and that we hope they will too. (1990, p. 87)

How Does Reading Aloud Support Reading Development?

Let us summarize. We have just discussed three important and powerful influences on a reader's ability to make meaning from printed language. These are the reader's background knowledge, the reader's language, and the reader's active engagement with the material being read. Reading aloud to your child can contribute to each of these.

❖ Reading aloud develops background knowledge.

How do we build background knowledge? Parents can provide experiences for children that build their knowledge of the world and will enable them to understand texts they later encounter in school and other settings. Take your child to the zoo. Take your child to museums. Explore natural settings—the ocean, national parks, your backyard. Talk about what you see. *Read to your child*. More can be explored in books than we will ever have a chance to experience firsthand. In books, children can travel the world, examine insects, explore the planets, visit a rain forest, construct a building, and much more.

❖ Reading aloud from a variety of books supports language development.

How do children acquire the language that will enable them to make sense of the formal language of books? Parents can read aloud to their children from many and varied books. Read some books over and over again. Read informational books, alphabet books, predictable books, familiar storybooks, fairy tales, and more.

❖ Reading aloud can encourage active engagement with books.

Reading aloud books that have personal relevance and books that invite participation are excellent ways to encourage active engagement with books. Talk about books. Discuss how you are the same as and different from the characters in a story. Share personal experiences similar to those in the book. Point to pictures. Laugh at an author's words.

Reading is both a decoding process and a meaning-making process. The child who cannot figure out the words on a page will never know the wonder of reading. Likewise, the child who *can* figure out the words, but does not make any sense of them, will never know the wonder of reading. In this chapter, we emphasized the role that parents and other caregivers can play in supporting children's ability to make meaning. Chapter Three returns to the issue of the symbol system of printed language as we look at three understandings that support children's ability to deal with the written code.

References

Adams, M. J. (1990). *Beginning to Read: Thinking and Learning about Print.* Cambridge, MA: The MIT Press.

Bransford, J. D., & McCarrell, N. S. (1974). A sketch of a cognitive approach to comprehension. In W. B. Weimer & D. S. Palermo (Eds.), *Cognition and the Symbolic Processes.* Hillsdale, NJ: Erlbaum.

Fielding, L. G., & Pearson, P. D. (February 1994). Reading comprehension: What works. *Educational Leadership*, 62–68.

Merriam Webster's Collegiate Dictionary. (10th ed.). (1996). Springfield, MA: Merriam-Webster.

Oxford American Dictionary. (1980). New York: Oxford University Press.

Webster's New World Dictionary and Thesaurus. (1996). New York: Simon & Schuster.

Children's Books Cited

Balducci, R. (1992). *Walt Disney's Snow White and the Seven Dwarfs.* New York: Golden.

Berenstain, S. & Berenstain, J. (1985). *The Berenstain Bears Learn about Strangers.* New York: Random House.

Bond, M. (1973). *Paddington Bear.* New York: Random House.

Brown, M. (1985). *Arthur's Tooth.* New York: Trumpet.

Cannon, J. (1997). *Stellaluna.* New York: Scholastic.

Carle, E. (1986). *The Very Hungry Caterpillar.* New York: Putnam.

Cauley, L. B. (1984). *The Town Mouse and the Country Mouse.* New York: G. P. Putnam's Sons.

Dodd, L. (1983). *Hairy Maclarey from Donaldson's Dairy.* New York: Trumpet.

Falconer, E. (1994). *The House That Jack Built.* Nashville, TN: Ideals.

Fichter, G. (1993). *Starfish, Seashells, and Crabs.* New York: Western Publishing.

Freeman, D. (1968). *Corduroy.* New York: Viking.

Galdone, P. (1983). *The Gingerbread Boy.* New York: Clarion.

Galdone, P. (1985). *The Little Red Hen.* Boston: Houghton Mifflin.

Gordon, J. R. (1991). *Six Sleepy Sheep.* Honesdale, PA: Boyd Mills.

Heller, R. (1992). *How to Hide an Octopus.* New York: Grosset & Dunlap.

Hill, E. (1985). *Spot Goes to the Beach.* New York: G. P. Putnam's Sons.

Hill, E. (1987). *Spot Goes to the Farm.* New York: G. P. Putnam's Sons.

Keats, E. J. (1981). *The Snowy Day.* New York: Viking.

Kellogg, S. (1986). *Pecos Bill.* New York: Scholastic.

Lowrey, J. S. (1970). *The Poky Little Puppy.* New York: Western Publishing.

Maifair, L. L. (1989). *I Can't Wait until Christmas.* New York: Western Publishing.

Martin, B., Jr. (1996). *Brown Bear, Brown Bear, What Do You See?* New York: Holt.

Martin, B., Jr. (1997). *Polar Bear, Polar Bear, What Do You Hear?* New York: Holt.

McDonald, M. (1990). *Is This a House for Hermit Crab?* New York: Orchard.

Numeroff, L. J. (1985). *If You Give a Mouse a Cookie.* New York: Harper & Row.

Reasoner, C. (1995). *Who's in the Sea?* New York: Price Stern Sloan.

Rounds, G. (1992). *The Three Little Pigs and the Big Bad Wolf.* New York: Trumpet.

Savage, S. (1994). *Animals under Cover.* New York: Simon & Schuster.

Sendak, M. (1962). *Chicken Soup with Rice.* New York: HarperTrophy.

Slepian, J., & Seidler, A. (1967). *The Hungry Thing.* New York: Scholastic.

Talkington, B. (1993). *Winnie the Pooh's Halloween.* New York: Disney.

Westcott, N. (1988*). I Know an Old Lady Who Swallowed a Fly.* New York: Cartwheel.

Wood, A. (1983). *The Napping House.* San Diego: Harcourt Brace Javonovich.

Zelinksy, P. O. (1986). *Rumpelstiltskin.* New York: Scholastic.

Chapter Three

Working with a Symbol System

*I*n Chapter Two we asked you to decode sentences written in languages other than English. We would like you to try a few more in this chapter. Please decode these written messages:

רֹאשׁ־הַשָּׁנָה הוּא חַג לִכְבוֹד הַהַתְחָלָה
שֶׁל הַשָּׁנָה הַחֲדָשָׁה.

Hebrew

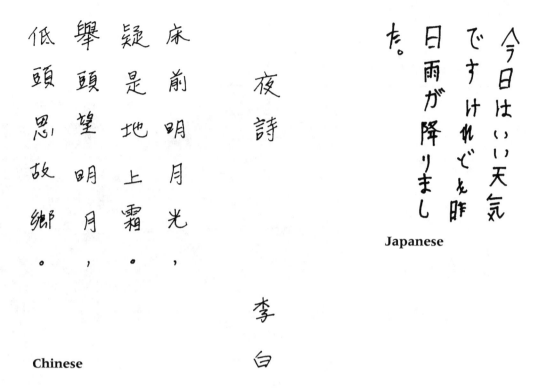

Japanese

Chinese

Did you have more difficulty this time? Were you even able to make an attempt at any of the examples? Unless you have had some exposure to these written languages, you likely were unable to generate the oral representation of the symbols. Decoding is difficult, if not impossible, if you are unfamiliar with the symbol system being used. And, being able to deal with the symbols of written language is crucial in reading. As we said in Chapter Two, reading involves dealing with the symbols of a written system as well as making meaning from our interactions with those symbols.

In this chapter, we discuss three understandings that are crucial to children's success in the decoding aspect of reading: knowledge of the symbols (the alphabet, for readers of English), concepts about print, and phonemic awareness.

Knowledge of the Alphabet

Research shows us that children who know the names and shapes of letters when formal reading instruction begins are more likely to experience success in learning to read than children who have had little experience with the alphabet. There are probably two reasons for this. One is that as important as one's language and background knowledge are (Chapter Two), they are not enough when learning to read. Children must become familiar with the symbols that are used in print; they must understand the special code that is used in their written language. The second reason is that knowledge of the alphabet suggests that children have had exposure to print. In many cases, it is the "tip of the iceberg." That is, children who know the alphabet know a great deal else in addition. They are likely to have had significant experiences with print. The more exposure to print, the more comfortable children are with engaging in reading activities themselves.

In order to learn to read, children must come to the realization that, in a world filled with visual stimuli, letters play a very special role. Further, they must recognize that a letter's orientation in space is important. Orientation is an issue unique to letters. A cookie is still a cookie regardless of the way you hold it—upside down, backwards, or sideways. But it matters what direction a letter is. Think of the letter "b." Rotate it and it becomes a "q." Flip it over sideways and it is a "d." Turn it another direction and it is a "p."

Children's familiarity with the alphabet typically begins with the alphabet song. Many toddlers can sing this song. Later, when children begin to notice letters and hear the names of the letters, they make a connection between the song they sing and the shapes they see. Children in homes rich in print (that is, where there are lots of books and other reading materials) have many opportunities to notice letters in their environment. They see letters on magazine covers and the morning newspaper. They see letters on the books on the coffee table and on clippings posted on the refrigerator. They see their parents using letters on market lists and on the checks they write at the checkout counter. They see letters on envelopes that come in the mail. They see letters in the books their parents read to them.

In the previous paragraph, we said that children in print-rich homes have many opportunities to notice letters in their environment. The word *notice* here is key. As important as it is to have a home filled with print, there is a difference between having print available and *noticing the print*. Exposure is not enough, educational researcher Marilyn Adams asserts in her book *Beginning to Read* (1990). Children must pay attention to the print. Parents are in a perfect position to inspire that attention.

We agree with Bernice Cullinan (1992), reading expert and former president of the International Reading Association, who states that it is not necessary to engage preschoolers in drills with alphabet flash cards. Rather, parents should respond to children's questions about print, telling them the names of letters when asked. They should ask children to find words on a page that start with the same letter as their names or as a letter they have inquired about. They should show them how to write their names and put their names on lunch boxes, clothing, books, and toys. Interesting books, games, and interactions with print will promote a familiarity with the alphabet.

Below are some suggestions for familiarizing your child with the letters of our written language. Perhaps you already engage in some of the activities recommended here. If not, we encourage you to make these simple and valuable additions to the time you spend with your child.

+ Purchase a set or two of magnetic letters from a local toy store. Put them on your refrigerator for both you and your child to play with. Have your child find the letter that begins his or her name. Spell your child's name with the letters. Move letters around and name them for your child. Write messages like "I love you" and read them to your child. Play with the letters.

+ Buy a set of plastic bathtub letters. Like the refrigerator magnetic letters, they will be used over and over again. Children love finding letters under the bubbles and sticking them to the walls above the tub. Play games with the letters: you call out a letter, your child finds it and sticks it to the wall; your child names a letter and you find it and stick it to the wall of the tub. Spell important words like "Mom," "Dad," and the child's name and tell the child what you have spelled.

+ Point out words or letters in the environment. When you walk around the neighborhood, stop at a stop sign and ask your child what it says. Chances are he or she will be able to tell you because of the familiar color and shape cues as well as the environmental cues (the street corner). Then pick up your child and have fun allowing him or her to touch and say each of the letters on the sign. Look at cereal boxes and comment on the letters. "Wow, that's big K, isn't it?" Notice the letters on storefronts and billboards.

✦ When you write a market list, let your child participate. Sit down at the kitchen table together. As your child helps you think of items to buy, let him or her observe you record those items on a piece of paper. Say each letter as you write it. "Yes, we need milk. M-I-L-K. What else do we need?"

✦ Give your child writing tools and paper for birthdays and holidays. Make sure that your home is full of pencils, crayons, markers, and paints and paintbrushes. Do not forget the sidewalk chalk! It is so much fun to write your name in huge colorful letters on the sidewalk.

✦ When you play in a sandbox, draw pictures and letters in the sand. Encourage your child to draw letters. Buy letter-shaped cookie cutters for use in the sand (or to make cookies).

✦ A favorite summertime activity for many children is water play. In addition to chasing each other with the hose, children enjoy filling buckets with water, dunking paintbrushes into the water, and writing letters all over the patio. Watch the letters disappear as the sun beats down on them.

✦ Decorate cupcakes with the initials of friends and family members. You can purchase decorative letters for your child to put on the cupcakes or buy a tube of decorator icing and have your child print the letters with you. Eating your way through these decorative letters is fun, too.

✦ When you make pancakes, form the letters of your child's name with the batter. Then read *Pancakes for Breakfast* by Tomie dePaola.

✦ Share alphabet books with your child. Many wonderful alphabet books are available in bookstores today. We recommend several and have made them a focus area in the book-sharing section of this book.

Concepts about Print

In order to learn to read, children must learn how books work. They must develop what educators call "concepts about print." Some of these concepts will seem pretty simple to you, but children only learn them if they have been read to a great deal and have had many opportunities to handle books. Concepts about print include knowing where the front of a book is and where the back of a book is, knowing how a book opens, knowing right side up from upside down and the top of a page from the bottom.

Simply reading to a child on your lap will help him or her learn basic concepts about print. As your child sees you turn the page, or better, participates in page turning, he or she gains a sense of how books work. Your child will see where a book begins and where it ends. Your child will see how you read from front to back. It is important that your child be close to you while

you read. Children lying in their beds across the room from a reading parent will observe far less than children who are snuggled in a parent's arms.

Some concepts about print require a bit more than just reading to a child in close proximity. For instance, children must eventually understand that it is the print—the words on the page—that is being read. The print, more than the pictures, carries the message. This is not readily apparent to children unless the adult who is reading occasionally points to the words while reading aloud. Pointing to words while reading also will support another concept about print: In English, we read from left to right and top to bottom. When you move your finger under a line you are reading and then lift your finger to move down to the next line of print, you are teaching your child directionality of text. There is no inherent reason why we read from left to right and top to bottom, so it must be learned. Did you know that the languages we asked you to decode at the beginning of this chapter are not read from left to right? They are read from right to left. Furthermore, although it is increasingly more common for Chinese characters to be recorded and read across the page, many Chinese newspapers, books, and greeting cards are read in columns. You start at the top of the right column, read down, then move left to the top of the next column and read down again. The Japanese example, too, reads top to bottom, beginning with the right column. The best way to teach directionality of print is through reading to your child and occasionally following the words with your finger.

These understandings about reading, these concepts about print, are very important in learning to read. Children who do not know how to handle a book when they begin kindergarten are at a serious disadvantage. In addition to lap

reading, pointing to words as you read, and encouraging your child to participate in page turning, here are some other ideas for supporting your child's developing understanding of how books and print work. If you try these activities,
not only will you build an understanding of the purpose and conventions of
print, but also you will emphasize the personal relevance print has in our lives.

+ Have a family message board. Let your child watch adults leave messages
  for one another. Read those messages aloud in your child's presence.
  Write messages to your child. On the day that you are going to visit relatives, write "Today we are going to Grandmother's house!" and show
  your child the message when he or she awakens in the morning.

+ Develop "to do" lists with your child. Let your child see that you begin at
  the top of a piece of paper, write from left to right, and then return to the
  left for the next line. Say the words slowly as you write them. You can
  revisit your list occasionally and let your child cross off what you have
  completed.

+ Give your child his or her own calendar. Record special events on the
  calendar. At the end of each day, talk about what your child did. Let him
  or her dictate what he or she wishes you to record for the day.

+ Have your child sit next to you at a table and dictate thank you notes for
  holiday and birthday gifts. Together, write letters to friends and relatives.

+ Make a book. Stack two or three pieces of paper, fold them in half, and
  staple the edge. Follow the model of a favorite story or create your own
  book. After a birthday party, you may wish to write about and illustrate
  the guests. "Joanna came to my party" could be on page one with a
  drawing of Joanna; "Oscar came to my party" could be on page two with
  an illustration, and so on.

+ Purchase some wordless picture books, such as *Rosie's Walk* by Pat Hutchins, *The Great Cat Chase* by Mercer Mayer, or *Peter Spier's Rain* by Peter
  Spier, and make up your own text to accompany the illustrations. Write
  your words or sentences on the book itself, or attach thin strips of paper
  to each page and write on these. Be sure to model good printing!

Phonemic Awareness

Reading experts have known for many years the value of familiarity with the
alphabet and the importance of children's developing concepts about print in
learning to read. In recent years, researchers have discovered another understanding that tremendously supports children's ability to work with the symbol system: **phonemic awareness.**

What is phonemic awareness? It is a particular insight about spoken language. As we pointed out in Chapter Two, a child's language abilities play a significant role in reading success. Researchers have discovered that a child's vocabulary and familiarity with a range of linguistic patterns enhance his or her reading abilities. But there is more to the language piece of the reading puzzle. We have discovered that a child's sensitivity to the sound basis of spoken language as separate from its meaning is highly instrumental in learning to read.

What do we mean by this? Consider the following: If you ask a preschooler which spoken word is longer, *train* or *caterpillar*, the typical response is *train*. This response reveals that, even though you asked which *word* is longer, the child is focusing on the meaning of the words rather than on the words themselves. If the focus is on meaning, of course, the answer is *train* because experience tells us that a train is much longer than a caterpillar.

Now consider this task: Ask a preschooler to tell you how many sounds are in the word *dog*. Many young children will respond to this question by barking! They know you are asking something about sounds and dogs. The logical reply, then, is to say "woof!" Other children simply will look at you with glazed eyes. They have no idea what you are asking. Young children use spoken language for communication—yes, this is the very purpose of language—and to ask them to shift their attention to examine or think about language itself is a challenge. When we ask children to reflect on spoken language separate from meaning, we get interesting responses.

Researchers and educators now know that a child's ability to think about language separate from its meaning is crucial in learning to read. In particular, it is a child's ability to think about the smallest building blocks of speech, the phonemes, that plays a key role in reading acquisition. This ability is called *phonemic awareness.*

Think about your speech for a moment. Say this sentence aloud: "I will read to my child every day." Pay attention to the meaning—please!—but also notice that the sentence is made up of a string of sounds. In fact, the sentence consists of 21 sounds! The word *I* has one sound; *will* is made up of three sounds (/w/-/i/-/l/); *read* is made up of three sounds (/r/-/ē/-/d/), and so on. Those small units of sound are called phonemes. In English, phonemes are sounds such as "mmmm" and "ssss" and "ffff." There are more than 40 phonemes in the English language. Some phonemes are represented by two letters such as "ch" and "sh." Some letters represent more than one phoneme, such as the "a" in cake and the "a" in cat. Phonemes are used in many combinations to create words. All words are made up of a sequence of phonemes. The word *ship*, for example, is made up of the sounds /sh/-/i/-/p/. The word *duck* is made up of the sounds /d/-/u/-/k/.

Why is it important that a child be aware that speech is made up of a sequence of small sounds? Here is the reason: In English, we use a written system (the alphabet) to record the smallest sounds of our language. The symbols we write represent the phonemes (such as /b/, /m/, /l/) of our spoken language. Not all written languages record the smallest sounds of speech. In fact, there are three modes of recording spoken language in the world today. Some written languages are logographs, some are syllabaries, and some are alphabets. In a logographic written system, idea-size units are recorded in print; each symbol (for the most part) represents an idea. Chinese, for example, is predominantly (though not exclusively) a logographic system. In order to be literate, readers must learn thousands of Chinese characters. Written Cherokee and some written Japanese are mostly records of syllable-size units of speech. Put simply, a two-syllable spoken word is written with two symbols. English and other alphabetic languages (for example, Spanish, French, German, Hmong) record the individual sounds of spoken language.

In learning to read an alphabetic language, it is extremely beneficial to realize that speech is made up of small units of sound. Think about it: If you do not know that your speech is made up of a sequence of sounds, then the logic of an alphabetic writing system is not apparent. To grasp our writing system, you must have the insight that speech is made up of sounds, and that it is these sounds we put into print. Print is language written down. What part of language? In English, it is the smallest parts of language, the phonemes. This is the alphabetic principle that eludes some children.

Developing phonemic awareness is no easy feat, particularly because when we speak wordscomeoutofourmouthslikethis. We do not pause between the individual words, let alone sounds, when speaking. So how do children become phonemically aware? It seems that children from linguistically stimulating homes are much more likely to enter school with a sensitivity to the phonemic basis of their language. This does not mean these children have parents who grunt and groan sounds to help children hear them as separate entities! Rather, they have parents who engage them in language play in which sounds are manipulated and in which attention is drawn to sounds. When adults help draw children's attention to the individual sounds of spoken language, we begin to build the foundation for later understanding of how letters represent sounds that build words.

The work of Louise Geller (1982a, 1982b) reveals that children spontaneously play with language sounds. Have you ever heard your child make up nonsense words that begin the same way as his or her name ("Toshi, Toshi, too, too, too!") or chant words that rhyme with his or her name ("Erica, Berica, Merica, Jerica!")? This ability to play with sounds in speech is the precursor to phonemic awareness. Parents should encourage such play with language, as nonsensical as it may seem.

Children's books can be very helpful in building phonemic awareness. Many stories draw attention to sounds, often in an amusing way. In *Cock-a-Doodle-Moo!* by Bernard Most, a cow tries to help a rooster who has lost his voice. The cow makes many attempts at saying "cock-a-doodle-doo" including

"mock-a-moodle-moo," "sock-a-noodle-moo," and "clock-a-doodle-moo." Children laugh at the cow's attempts, and you will find them saying "cock-a-doodle-doo" in their own silly ways, expanding on the author's work. What a wonderful way to focus children's attention on sounds!

Rhyming books are wonderful read-aloud books. Not only do they encourage predictions, but those predictions are based on finding words with similar sounds! In *Down by the Bay* by Raffi, a child asks, "Did you ever see a moose kissing a goose?" Listeners who are thinking about the story and noticing the sound element (the rhyme) in the story will be able to fill in the blank on another page: "Did you ever see a fly wearing a _____?" Did you say "shirt"? Probably not. You are sensitive to the sound play and probably responded "tie" because it rhymes with fly. How about this one: "Did you ever see a whale with a polka dot _____?" Did you guess "tail"? Many words would be logical in this silly story, but our choices narrow when we notice sounds, too.

When the two-year-old daughter of one of the authors listened to the story *Chicka Chicka Boom Boom,* by Bill Martin, Jr. and John Archambault, she loved the moment when her mother would read, "Skit skat skoodle doot. Flip flop flee." She would giggle and repeat, "Flip flop flee" and squeal, "Do dat 'gin, Mommy" ("Do that again, Mommy!"). Several years earlier, her then three-year-old brother, Peter, would grin and say "I like that part, Mommy" when read "Pit pat paddle pat, Pit pat waddle pat" in *The Tale of Tom Kitten* by Beatrix Potter. Why did they enjoy these phrases so much? Because they were enthralled with the way the authors played with sounds.

When reading aloud a book in which the author uses rhymes or alliterations ("Many mumbling mice are making midnight music . . . " in *Dr. Seuss's ABC*) or substitutes or adds sounds ("Happy hippopotamamas in their pretty pink pajamas . . . " in *The Happy Hippopotami* by Bill Martin, Jr.), take the time to point out what the author has done. Talk about what makes this book so fun. If your child is interested, do not hesitate to read the book or phrases from the book over and over again.

Here are some other ways to stimulate phonemic awareness:

✦ Capitalize on your child's natural interest in playing with sounds. When he or she makes up silly words or phrases, join in the fun. Make up your own silly words and phrases. Do not discourage nonsensical exploration of language.

✦ There are many songs that play with sounds. Like books, some rhyme. Others manipulate sounds in other ways. Remember the song "The Name Game"? "Shirley, Shirley, bo-ber-ley, bo-n-a-na fanna fo-fer-ley, fee fi mo-mer-ley, Shirley!" Children love this song, and the point of the song is sound play. You can sing the traditional song "The Corner Grocery Store" in the car on the way to the market with your children. The idea is to find rhymes for foods. "There was cheese, cheese, walkin' on its knees, in the corner grocery store." Name a food, and let your child try to think of a rhyme. Let him or her pick a food, and you try to think of a rhyme. In another traditional song, "Apples and Bananas," the vowel sounds are manipulated: "ape-ples and ba-nay-nays"; "ee-pples and bee-nee-nees"; "i-pples and bi-ni-nis"; and so on. There are many playful children's songs that you can enjoy together, while helping develop phonemic awareness at the same time.

✦ You also can play word games with your child. Guessing games often are popular with young children. How about an "I Spy" game? "I spy with my little eye something in the room that starts like this: /sh/. You put it on your foot. It is your sh___ (shoe). I spy with my little eye something in the sky that starts like this: /b/ (bird)."

✦ Poetry is useful for stimulating phonemic awareness. Many poems are constructed around the sounds in words—sounds are repeated, rhyme is used, and other play with sounds is emphasized. In "Antonio," a poem found in *The Random House Book of Poetry for Children* (Prelutsky, 1983), a man named Antonio is tired of living "alonio" and wants to take a wife for his "ownio." The humor in this poem comes in part from the "io" added to the end of the final word in many lines. Poetry can help to develop a child's sensitivity to the sound basis of language. You will notice that we have included in the activities section of this book many suggestions of poetry for you to share with your child.

✦ Interestingly, a child's knowledge of nursery rhymes has been shown to be related to later reading achievement. There are apparently two reasons for this. First, it represents, again, the "tip of the iceberg." Children who know nursery rhymes probably come from print-rich, literate homes where they have many experiences with books. Second, nursery rhymes support the development of phonemic awareness because of the rhyme element and other sound play.

✦ Encourage any attempts at writing that your child initiates. If your children make random marks on a paper as they "write" a message, celebrate! They understand that their thoughts can be communicated through writing. If they use random letters, celebrate! They know those symbols in particular carry their message. If they use letters that begin to match the sounds in the words of their message, recognize the tremendous achievement they have made. Early spelling attempts—unconventional as they may be—represent a child's growing insight that it is the small units of sound in speech that we have chosen to put on paper in our written system. This is a significant, important step in literacy development!

Some parents worry that if they allow their children to misspell words they are building a bad habit that will last through the school years. This is not true. Reading researchers agree that young children's unconventional spellings are a positive step in their literacy development. Young children, preschoolers,

and kindergarteners should be given many opportunities to create spellings. Doing so reveals that they are engaged in thinking about the sounds of their language and are developing an understanding of our written system.

A final word about phonemic awareness is needed. Many people confuse phonemic awareness with phonics. They think it is a fancy new name for an old idea. But phonemic awareness is not phonics. Phonemic awareness is a person's understanding that the stream of words that comes out of his or her mouth consists of a sequence of individual sounds that have been put together in a certain order. Phonics, on the other hand, refers to an instructional strategy for teaching the symbols that represent sounds. Until an individual knows that speech is made up of a sequence of sounds, phonics instruction is problematic. Imagine the frustration and sense of failure children experience who are asked to "sound out" a written word when they do not even know that words are made up of sounds. In years past, some of those children who struggled with phonics instruction likely lacked the phonemic awareness foundation that made phonics instruction logical. Today's kindergarten and primary grade teachers build their phonics instruction with their students' developing phonemic awareness in mind. Parents can play a significant role in building this foundation by providing linguistically stimulating home environments that both stretch meaningful language and playfully manipulate the sounds of language.

We have discussed the importance of three understandings that support children's success in working with the symbol system of written language: alphabet knowledge, concepts about print, and phonemic awareness. The good news is that the development of each one of these understandings is facilitated through experiences with books. Remember, though, that understanding the symbol system is only one piece of what it means to be a reader. Meaning making is the heart of the reading experience. We hope that you will spend many happy hours enjoying books with your children for the information and entertainment they provide as well as for the skills they can help develop.

References

Adams, M. J. (1990). *Beginning to Read: Thinking and Learning about Print*. Cambridge, MA: The MIT Press.

Cullinan, B. (1992). *Read to Me: Raising Kids Who Love to Read*. New York: Scholastic.

Geller, L. G. (1982a). Grasp of meaning in children: Theory into practice. *Language Arts, 59*, 429–444.

Geller, L. G. (1982b). Linguistic consciousness-raising: Child's play. *Language Arts, 59*, 120–125.

Children's Books Cited

dePaola, T. (1978). *Pancakes for Breakfast*. San Diego: Harcourt Brace Jovanovich.

Hutchins, P. (1968). *Rosie's Walk*. New York: Macmillan.

Martin, B., Jr., & Archambault, J. (1989). *Chicka Chicka Boom Boom*. New York: Scholastic.

Martin, B., Jr. (1991). *The Happy Hippopotami*. San Diego: Harcourt Brace.

Mayer, M. (1974). *The Great Cat Chase*. New York: Scholastic.

Most, B. (1996). *Cock-a-Doodle-Moo!* San Diego: Harcourt Brace.

Potter, B. (1987). *The Tale of Tom Kitten*. New York: Penguin.

Prelutsky, J. (1983). *The Random House Book of Poetry for Children*. New York: Random House.

Raffi. (1990). *Down by the Bay*. New York: Crown.

Seuss, Dr. (1963). *Dr. Seuss's ABC*. New York: Random House.

Spier, P. (1982). *Peter Spier's Rain*. New York: Doubleday.

For Further Reading

Yopp, H. K. & Yopp, R. H. (1996). *Oo-pples and Boo-noo-noos: Songs and Activities for Phonemic Awareness*. Orlando: Harcourt Brace School Publishers.

Chapter Four

Selecting and Sharing Children's Literature

Books are keys to
    wisdom's treasure;
Books are gates to
    lands of pleasure;
Books are paths that
    upward lead;
Books are friends,
    Come, let us read.

—Emilie Poulsson

*W*e hope we have convinced you of the powerful role you play in your children's reading development. By bringing books into your home and into your children's lives, you are setting the stage for successful reading. In this chapter, we will discuss what it is that parents should know about children's literature, including types of children's literature and how to select children's literature; we will offer suggestions for sharing children's literature.

The Variety of Children's Literature

A variety of genres, or types, of children's literature are available in the marketplace today. For reasons discussed later in this chapter, it is important that your child experience many types of books. Experts often classify literature in the following categories:

✦ **Picture books** are those in which the text and illustrations combine to tell a story. The text is minimal, and the illustrations provide information not stated in the text. The term *picture books* can cover a wide variety of children's books, including alphabet books, counting books, wordless books, concept books (such as books that teach colors or shapes), and storybooks. They may be fiction or nonfiction. Although picture books are most commonly thought of as appropriate for young children, they also can be enjoyed by older children and adults.

✦ **Traditional literature** consists of folktales, fables, legends, and myths. While there are differences among these types of traditional literature, they have in common that they are born of oral tradition. *Little Red Riding Hood, The Hare and the Tortoise,* and *The Town Mouse and the Country Mouse* are familiar examples of traditional literature.

✦ **Nonfiction books** include informational books and biographies. Informational books are an important part of a child's library, and serve as excellent resources for eager, questioning minds. Biographies are true accounts of individuals who really lived or are living. Many well-written and beautifully illustrated nonfiction books are available for young children today.

✦ **Modern fantasy** and **science fiction** are stories that involve a violation of reality. These are the books in which animals talk, dinosaurs live in modern times, toys come to life, and miniature people live in attics. Science fiction is often distinguished from fantasy by its use of technology, computers, and robots.

✦ Writers of **contemporary realistic fiction** use their imaginations to tell stories that really could happen and are set in modern times. The word "realistic" does not mean that the story is true; it means that everything about the story—the plot, the setting, the characters—is realistic. Popular types of realistic fiction include humorous stories, animal stories, sports stories, school stories, and mysteries.

✦ **Historical fiction** allows children to experience events of times past. Stories can be fictionalized accounts of real people and events in our history, or they can describe the experiences of a fictional character set in a real time in history. Often these books are rich in facts and provide the reader with a personal view of a past period.

✦ **Poetry** is characterized by economy of language, attention to sound, and emotional impact. Three types of poetry books are available for children: comprehensive anthologies, collections of poems written by a single poet or related to a single theme, and picture book versions of single poems.

Today's families are fortunate. We live in a time when bookstores and libraries abound with excellent literature for children. Now, more than ever, parents can find high-quality books in each of the genres just discussed to share with their children. The next section offers suggestions for selecting from among the thousands of books available.

Selecting Children's Literature

One way to begin selecting children's literature is to look for award-winning books and authors. Two of the best-known awards are the Caldecott Medal and the Newbery Medal, both presented annually by the American Library Association. The Caldecott Medal is given to the artist of the most distinguished picture book published in the United States. Several additional books may be cited as worthy of attention and named Caldecott Honor books. The Newbery Medal is awarded to the author of the most distinguished contribution to American literature for children. Newbery Honor books also are named. Newbery award-winning books often are most appropriate for older children. Caldecott and Newbery award-winning books are easy to locate, as lists are readily available at libraries and bookstores, and the books often are housed in specially marked sections or shelves.

Other less well known awards include the Laura Ingalls Wilder Award, which is presented by the American Library Association to an author or illustrator who has made a lasting contribution to children's literature. The Batchelder Award is presented by the American Library Association to the publisher of an outstanding book originally published outside the United States and subsequently translated and published in the United States. The Hans Christian Andersen Prize is an international children's book award and is selected biannually by the International Board on Books for Young People.

Some awards are targeted for children's books related to particular content or themes. For example, the Coretta Scott King Award is given to an African American author and an African American illustrator for outstanding inspirational and educational contributions to children's literature. The Association of Jewish Libraries awards are presented to books that have made outstanding contributions to the field of Jewish literature. The Catholic Book Award is given to books with Christian and psychological values. The Orbis Pictus Award is given to an outstanding work of nonfiction for children by the National Council of Teachers of English. Librarians can direct you to resources that provide information about the awards and the recipients of those awards.

Award-winning books have been selected carefully by committees made up of individuals with expertise in children's literature; however, the members of those committees are not experts on *your* child! Therefore, although we recommend that you seek out award-winning literature, we encourage you to keep the interests, attitudes, and experiences of your child in mind. You should select books that will capture and hold your child's attention. What topics will bring your child enjoyment? What books are likely to be asked for again and again by your child? What is important in your child's life?

We also suggest that you ask friends, teachers, and librarians for recommendations. And consider exploring magazines and other resources that review children's literature. Libraries house these resources in their children's section, and librarians can direct you to them.

Another source of information is the internet. A number of book sellers are on-line, and finding books is quite simple. Searches may be conducted by title, author, and topic, or in a variety of other ways, including award winners and recent best-sellers. Often, considerable information is provided on-line. Along with information such as publisher, date of publication, and cost of a book, you might find reviews of the book. Some reviews are written by authorities in children's literature, and some are written by members of the public who have read the book and wish to comment on it. If your child has been particularly interested in a book, search for others by the same author. If your child has had an experience you wish to address with books, conduct a topic search. You and your child may wish to browse on-line bookstores together!

Of course, another source of quality literature is this book. We have listed more than 400 works of excellent children's literature. Our selections should keep you busy for quite some time!

Whatever your source, you should consider the following questions when selecting books for your child:

> Does the author avoid stereotyping based on gender, race, culture, and profession?
>
> Do the illustrations complement the text?
>
> If fiction, does the story have universal or personal appeal?
>
> If nonfiction, is the information accurate and current?

Finally, in selecting books for your child, consider what you have learned in this book about reading development.

❖ *Choose books that support and extend your child's experiences with and knowledge of the world.*

Select books that draw on familiar concepts or experiences. These will allow your child to make meaningful connections with the book. If you have recently visited a zoo, consider a book about zoos. If you have been stargazing, choose a book about the night sky. Children's personal experiences—their relevant background knowledge—will enhance their understanding of the books you read to them.

Conversely, look for books that will broaden your children's knowledge of the world. Your children cannot possibly experience everything there is to experience, but you can expand their background knowledge by sharing books about the unfamiliar. The child who has been read *Animals under Cover* by Stephen Savage and *How to Hide a Meadow Frog* by Ruth Heller has built concepts about how life forms protect themselves from predators. Children who have perused a book on animal skeletons will bring more to the experience when they read about the animal kingdom in later years.

Share multicultural books. Listening to the customs, experiences, hopes, and dreams of people from diverse cultures not only will broaden your child's understanding of the world—building a knowledge base that he or she can access when reading books later—but also will increase your child's sensitivity to and appreciation for people of other cultural groups. It will help him or her appreciate the universality of the human experience.

❖ *Choose books that promote language development.*

Remember that your child's language strongly influences his or her ability to read. Reading to your child can expand your child's vocabulary. Just as reading *Animals under Cover* and *How to Hide a Meadow Frog* can build certain conceptual understandings, so too can reading these books provide your child with vocabulary that supports that knowledge. You will notice the words "camouflage," "prey," and "predator" becoming a part of your child's vocabulary as he or she attempts to describe and explain our world. Vocabulary is a powerful determinant of ability to understand text.

Reading to your child also can provide important experiences with a variety of language patterns. Include predictable books in your child's library because they can expand a child's understanding of language as he or she figures out what makes sense based on the ideas as well as the language of the book.

Select books that use simple sentences as well as those that incorporate more complex sentence structures. As we noted in Chapter Two, the language of books is different from the language of everyday speech. Giving your child opportunities to listen to more formal and more complex language structures prepares him or her for future reading experiences.

Include all literary genres in your selections. Children benefit from experiences with picture books, informational books, modern fantasies, science fiction, contemporary realistic fiction, traditional literature, historical fiction, and poetry. This variety not only provides for much enjoyment, but also develops familiarity with the many types of books your child will encounter in later years. Experience with a variety of genres also helps expand children's vocabulary and develop an understanding of different text structures. Exposing your child to fiction, for example, helps build an understanding that stories are made up of characters, settings, and plots. Research shows that young children often have a very good sense of story. Children are less comfortable, however, with the variety of informational text structures: cause-effect, sequencing, comparison, description, and problem-solution. Providing children with experiences with these text structures is important in their development as readers. In fact, there are educators who blame early lack of exposure to informational books for the problems some children have reading content texts in upper elementary grades. Be sure to include a variety of genres in your text selections.

❖ Choose books that are likely to promote active engagement.

A child's ability to make meaning during reading is enhanced when the child is actively engaged in thinking about what he or she reads. Therefore, select books that encourage active participation. Predictable books that stimulate chanting along with the author's words, manipulative books that require lifting a flap or pulling a tab, and books on topics of high interest or that answer questions your child has asked or that relate to an experience he or she has had promote active engagement.

❖ Choose books that build alphabet knowledge and phonemic awareness.

Remember the importance of familiarity with the letters and sounds of the alphabet in learning to read. And recall that the understanding that words are made up of sequences of individual sounds is important to reading success. Include alphabet books in your selections, as well as books that play with the sounds of language, such as rhyming books, books with alliterations, and books that include nonsense words created by moving sounds around. Many Dr. Seuss books are great examples of language play.

Sharing Children's Literature

Most of your shared reading experiences with your child will involve simply picking up a book and reading it to him or her. Be sure to select a comfortable place at a time when there are no competing activities. Consider establishing a routine time for reading (such as bedtime), but do not restrict yourself to this time. Take advantage of other opportunities throughout the day. One afternoon, one of the author's children stood on a swivel chair to reach something from a shelf. His aunt who was with him at the time stopped what she was doing and quickly grabbed the humorous book *Officer Buckle and Gloria* by Peggy Rathman to read. (In the story, Officer Buckle offers safety tips, one of which is "Never stand on a swivel chair.") This book and his aunt's playful yet pointed reading of it on this occasion left a lasting impression about safety and about books.

While reading to your child, be sure to pursue any invitations your child extends to discuss what is being read. Do not view questions and comments as interruptions that are to be shushed; view them as signs of your child's involvement in the book and as opportunities to respond to your child's interests and expand his or her knowledge. Ask thought-provoking questions. Occasionally elaborate on concepts and on word meanings. Sometimes draw attention to print features.

Take your cues from your child on how much time to spend reading. Some young children will sit and listen for long periods, others for briefer periods that you will want to work slowly to extend. Pay attention to which books interest your child. Observe your child's nonverbal responses to the nature and duration of your conversations about books. If he or she squirms or appears not to be paying attention, perhaps you are talking too much and should get back to reading!

We hope that you will read several books to your child every day, share books of every genre, and reread favorites as many times as your child re-

quests over the years. You can enhance the reading experience occasionally by planning for three phases of reading: before reading, during reading, and after reading. In other words, there are activities you might engage in before you actually begin reading the book. These prereading activities will arouse your child's curiosity or help your child see connections between what he or she already knows and what he or she is about to hear. They help to set the stage for reading. Then, there are things that you can do during the actual reading experience that will increase comprehension, focus your child's attention, and promote enjoyment and participation in the reading experience. Finally, there are activities you can engage in that will extend the learning experience after you have closed the cover of the book. We follow this before reading–during reading–after reading model in the activities section of this book.

Any activity you engage in should be done with your child in mind. When your son or daughter enters school, you want him or her not only to be ready to participate in school reading instruction but also to be eager to enter the world of books. Developing children who can but will not read is an outcome no one desires. We began this chapter with one of our favorite poems. We think the last stanza sums up the attitude we hope all children have as school beckons.

> *Books are friends,*
> *Come, let us read.*

Children's Books Cited

Heller, R. (1995). *How to Hide a Meadow Frog*. New York: Grosset & Dunlap.
Savage, S. (1994). *Animals under Cover*. New York: Little Simon.
Rathman, P. (1995). *Officer Buckle and Gloria*. New York: Scholastic.

For Further Reading

Kobrin, B. (1995). *Eyeopeners II: Children's Books to Answer Children's Questions about the World around Them*. New York: Scholastic.
Miller-Lachmann, L. (1992). *Our Family, Our Friends, Our World: An Annotated Guide to Significant Multicultural Books for Children and Teenagers*. New Providence, NJ: Bowker.
Trelease, J. (1989). *The New Read-Aloud Handbook*. New York: Penguin.

Part II

A Year's Worth of Reading

The Book-Sharing Experience

*T*his section presents sixty book-sharing experiences, enough for one a week for an entire year with eight additional Book Shares for special occasions. We found these experiences among the most special and memorable we had with our own children. We hope you find them as special.

Each Book Share features a work of children's literature that will be the focus of the sharing experience. Book Share 1, for instance, is built around *The Napping House* by Audrey Wood. We start each Book Share with a quote. This is our way of showing there are a great many people who view reading and literature as important and enjoyable. Following the quote is information about the book to be shared. The quote and the information about the book are for you, the parent or caregiver. They are not intended to be read to your child.

You are then supplied with suggestions on where the book-sharing experiences might take place (for example, outdoors or in the kitchen) and the materials that are needed during this sharing. Some activities use art supplies, some involve cooking ingredients, and some require no materials at all. Next, we suggest activities for each of the three phases of shared reading we discussed in Chapter Four: before reading, during reading, and after reading. In other words, we offer activities to engage in before reading the featured book begins to pique your child's interest, stimulate questions, or build his or her background knowledge. We provide suggestions for what to do as the literature is read in order to encourage your child's participation in the reading, to facilitate comprehension, or to focus his or her attention on some aspect of the book.

Then, we outline some enjoyable experiences to share after the book is completed. Along with the featured book, we suggest an additional six books that center around a theme associated with the featured book or are by the same author. We encourage you to read aloud these additional books throughout the week.

To use *Ready for Reading* to its fullest advantage, you will need to purchase four books of poetry for children. As we discussed in Chapter Three, reading poetry to children, especially poetry that rhymes or plays with sounds, is a powerful way to develop phonemic awareness. Each Book Share will suggest seven poems to read to your child throughout the week. These poems come from the following four books: *Where the Sidewalk Ends* by Shel Silverstein, *The Random House Book of Poetry for Children* by Jack Prelutsky, *The Real Mother Goose* by Blanche Fisher Wright, and *The New Kid on the Block* by Jack Prelutsky.

You will notice that we recommend some books and poems be read two, three, or even more times during the year. We have done this deliberately. Good literature should be experienced often. Parents who are old-timers at reading to children are well aware that children ask, and often demand, that old favorites be read again, and again, . . . and again.

The first four chapters of *Ready for Reading* stress that the book-sharing experiences you have with your child are important as they can specifically enhance children's reading development in significant ways. For each book, we identify the value of the book selection and accompanying activities, using the following key:

+ By sharing all the books introduced, but especially those labeled "Personal Value" or "Special Moments," you will help children develop a love of and appreciation for literature. Children will see that reading can be truly rewarding and that it is an important part of their lives.

+ By using the books labeled "Predictable and Pattern," you will help children become aware of how words work in text. Children will develop an understanding of the way sentences and stories are put together.

+ Through the use of the books labeled "Alphabet," you will help children become aware of letter names and letter sounds. This familiarity with the symbol system of our language will be helpful to your child's reading development.

+ Through the sharing of books labeled "Phonemic Awareness," you will help children develop the insight that speech is made up of a sequence of small sounds. Children will become sensitive to the sound basis of our language and build the ability to manipulate these sounds in speech. This is an important component of getting children ready for reading.

You will want to pick and choose from the Book Shares those most appropriate for your family in any given week. In fact, picking and choosing is at the heart of *Ready for Reading*. We have presented you with 60 featured books and suggested how you might share them. What we have presented truly are suggestions. Please feel comfortable reading any of these books with your children at any time and modifying and changing the activities so they best fit the circumstances and the needs of your children. If there is snow on the ground, the idea of reading *How a Seed Grows* and then working in the garden probably will not be appealing. Sitting in a warm kitchen, having milk and cookies while enjoying *If You Give a Mouse a Cookie* might make a great deal more sense. Also, although we suggest comments that you might make before, during, or after reading, these are simply to provide you with a flavor of the types of interactions we encourage you to have with your child. Please do not feel that you need to quote us directly!

To help you select a Book Share, we have provided several indices after Book Share 60. You will find a Book Share Literacy Focus Index, which allows you to identify quickly Book Shares according to category: personal value, special moments, predictable and pattern, alphabet, and phonemic awareness. The Book Share Subject Index enables you to find Book Shares related to various topics, such as birthdays, nature, or holidays. We also include a Book Share Materials Index so that you may quickly determine which Book Shares involve food, which involve toys or stuffed animals, and so on.

Although *Ready for Reading* is directed primarily to parents of preschoolers, these book-sharing experiences may be engaged in with children well into their kindergarten or first-grade year as they provide excellent support for the literacy activities taking place in the classroom.

We hope you can place shelves or a bookcase in your child's room so that all his or her books can be displayed. You may wish to purchase the featured books so that they can become part of your child's permanent library. These are books you are likely to share over and over with your child. You also will find your son or daughter returning to these books time after time and even year after year. As he or she develops independence in reading, these books will become old friends that are read repeatedly. The six additional children's books we recommend for each week almost always can be found at a local library.

Now, it is time to sit down with your child and share a great book. Look through the Book Shares and select one for this week. You are about to begin a very special year. We wish you good reading.

Recommended Books of Poetry

Prelutsky, J. (1984). *The New Kid on the Block.* New York: Greenwillow Books.
Prelutsky, J. (1983). *The Random House Book of Poetry for Children.* New York: Random House.
Silverstein, S. (1974). *Where the Sidewalk Ends.* New York: Harper and Row.
Wright, B. F. (1944). *The Real Mother Goose.* New York: Checkerboard Press.

Quick Book Share Guide

Book Share 1

*Lively books, read with lively interest, leave strong
and lasting recollections.*
    —Walter Bagehot

Title: *The Napping House*

Author: Audrey Wood

Illustrator: Don Wood

Publisher: Harcourt Brace

Summary: This book has to be considered a classic in the predictable and pattern category. It is a story children love to have read to them and parents love to read. *The Napping House* should be read a number of times, especially on rainy days. It begins in a cozy house with a gentle rain falling outside—a perfect time for napping! Granny naps first. A child falls asleep on top of her. They are joined by a dog, cat, mouse, and flea. Quite a crowd is in the bed. While the others slumber, the flea bites the mouse setting off a chain reaction that awakens everyone to a sunny, beautiful day.

Key: Predictable and Pattern

✦ **Setting and Materials Needed:** The book sharing takes place best at nap or bedtime. The only materials needed are six stuffed animals ranging in size from large to small. It would be great if this could be read on a rainy day.

✦ **Before Reading Activity:** Show your child the cover of the book and read the title. Say, "I wonder what is going on here? Let's find out." You will need to say little else.

✦ **During Reading Activity:** As you read the book make sure your child can see and appreciate every picture. Discuss the pictures if your child wants to but you both may prefer simply to enjoy the gentle, wonderful story. Then say, "Do you want to hear it again?" You know what the answer will be. Read it again and put special emphasis on the words that describe how each person or animal sleeps. For example, stress "snoozing," "dozing," "snoring."

◆ **After Reading Activity:** When you have finished reading the story a second time, gather up the stuffed animals and put the largest at the foot of the bed. Read the story again but instead of a snoring granny say "a snoring teddy" or the name of whatever stuffed animal you choose. Continue reading the book and stacking the animals as best you can.

◆ **Poetry Partners:** "Mice," "The Bat," "The Sloth," "The Camel," "The Camel's Complaint," "The Hippopotamus," and "The Oliphaunt" in *The Random House Book of Poetry for Children.*

◆ **Related Books:** *King Bidgood's in the Bathtub, Heckedy Peg, Little Penguin's Tale, Bird Song,* and *Elbert's Bad Word* all by Audrey Wood; and *The Baby's Bedtime Book* by Kay Chorao.

Book Share 2

Read at whim! read at whim!
—Randall Jarrell

Title: *We're Going on a Bear Hunt*

Author: Michael Rosen

Illustrator: Helen Oxenbury

Publisher: Little Simon

Summary: In this rhythmical book, a family goes on a bear hunt. The father, mother, and three children make their way through long wavy grass (swishy, swashy), a deep cold river (splash, splosh), and other exciting, scary, noisy places before they come to a narrow, gloomy cave. They're not afraid—until they see the object of their search, a bear! They race back home, retracing their path, and jump into bed together, pulling the covers over their heads. They vow never to go on a bear hunt again.

Key: Predictable and Pattern, Phonemic Awareness

◆ **Setting and Materials Needed:** Read the story in your child's bedroom, in a sitting position (since you will need to pound your feet). Before you read this book to your child, secretly hide a teddy bear under a blanket somewhere in your house.

◆ **Before Reading Activity:** Look at the picture on the cover of the book. Tell your child that this family is going to hunt for a bear.

◆ **During Reading Activity:** As you read the book, act out some of the movements. Stomp your feet on the ground as you move through the tall grass. Make swimming motions with your arms as you cross the river. Lift your feet high as you read about moving through the mud, Encourage your child to participate in the reading of the sounds made at each point in the journey: as the family walks through the grass ("Swishy swashy! Swishy swashy!"), wades through the river ("Splash splosh! Splash splosh! Splash splosh!"), and so on.

✦ **After Reading Activity:**   Suggest to your child that the two of you go on a bear hunt through your home. Chant the words from the book as you go. The words are easy to remember, so you will not need to carry the book. You might even want to make up your own words as you move from room to room. Eventually, go into the room where you have hidden the bear. Notice the lump under the blanket and say, "What's that?" Lift the blanket and exclaim, "It's a bear!!" Hurriedly retrace your steps through the house until you land in your child's bed where you pull the covers over your heads.

Your child will probably wish to repeat this activity. You may hide the bear in the same location or find a new location. Also, you may decide together that you will chase your child with the bear all the way back to his or her bedroom once you discover the bear.

After engaging in this activity, you and your child may wish to make binoculars for future hunts. Roll two pieces of paper into tubes, staple them side by side, attach a ribbon so the "binoculars" can be hung around your necks. Our children spent many hours using these binoculars to hunt imaginary creatures.

✦ **Poetry Partners:**   "Dogs and Cats and Bears and Bats," "Grandpa Bear's Lullaby," "Polar Bear," "Feather or Fur," and "Adventures of Isabel" in *The Random House Book of Poetry for Children;* "I'm Bold, I'm Brave" and "The Cave Beast Greets a Visitor" in *The New Kid on the Block.*

✦ **Related Books:**   *Where's the Bear?* by Charlotte Pomerantz; *"I Don't Care!" Said the Bear* by Colin West; *Goldilocks and the Three Bears* by James Marshall; *Every Autumn Comes the Bear* by Jim Arnosky; *Blueberries for Sal* by Robert McCloskey; *Little Rabbit Foo-Foo* by Michael Rosen.

Book Share 3

*The best guide to books is a book itself. It clasps
hands with a thousand other books.*
    —Maurice Francis Egan

Title: *Green Eggs and Ham*

Author: Dr. Seuss

Publisher: Random House Beginner Book

Summary: This is the number one selling Dr. Seuss book. Sam-I-am
tries to get a larger, older friend to eat green eggs and ham. The friend naturally is reluctant but Sam-I-am is persistent. He tries to get his friend to
eat green eggs and ham in a variety of settings, from in a house with a
mouse to in a box with a fox. The answer is always "no" until the friend is
worn down by the persistent Sam-I-am and finally agrees to try them—and
likes them!

Key: Predictable and Pattern

✦ **Setting and Materials Needed:** The book sharing should take place at the
kitchen or dining room table. You will be making, no surprise, green eggs and
ham at the end of this activity. You will need the necessary ingredients and
some green food coloring.

✦ **Before Reading Activity:** This activity should take place before the breakfast meal. As you sit at the table say, "How would you like some green eggs
and ham for breakfast?" Your child's answer will probably be a fairly predictable, "No!" Then say, "Well, I am going to read you a book about green
eggs and ham. Maybe the book will change your mind about green eggs and
ham." If your child says "yes" to the question then say, "Good, but before I
make green eggs and ham, let me read you a book called *Green Eggs and Ham*.
Let's see if it sounds like a tasty breakfast."

✦ **During Reading Activity:** As you read the story, make a slight pause each time you meet a rhyming word. For example, when reading, "Would you eat them in a box? Would you eat them with a [*slight pause*] fox?" Also, two or three times during your reading, stop and ask, "Do you think he will try the green eggs and ham this time?"

✦ **After Reading Activity:** This is probably one of the more obvious after reading activities. Make two breakfasts. One with, and one without, green food coloring. It is best when you scramble the eggs. A very small amount of food coloring in the eggs will usually do the trick. Give your child the choice of either meal, or give each of you a green and a nongreen sample. Enjoy eating the food. Try a few bites where you each close your eyes to see if the green food tastes any different. Read *Green Eggs and Ham* again.

✦ **Poetry Partners:** "Pancake?" "Melinda May," "The Silver Fish," "Peanut-Butter Sandwich," "With His Mouth Full of Food," "Recipe for a Hippopotamus Sandwich," and "Me-Stew" in *Where the Sidewalk Ends*.

✦ **Related Books:** *Benny Bakes a Cake* by Eve Rice; *I Know an Old Lady Who Swallowed a Fly* by Nadine B. Westcott; and *The Cat in the Hat, The Cat in the Hat Comes Back, Dr. Seuss's ABC,* and *Dr. Seuss's Sleep Book* all by Dr. Seuss.

Book Share 4

*The sight of the cover of a book one has previously read
retains, woven into the letters of its title, the moonbeams
of a far-off summer night.*
—Marcel Proust

Title: *Goodnight Moon*

Author: Margaret Wise Brown

Illustrator: Clement Hurd

Publisher: Harper

Summary: This is a wonderful bedtime book for children. It is the story of a young bunny in bed saying goodnight to everything that can be said goodnight to. In the room, there is a quiet old lady "whispering 'hush.' " The book concludes with the room warm and comfortably dark and the young bunny falling asleep while saying, "Goodnight stars, goodnight air, goodnight noises everywhere." *Goodnight Moon* is a book that is meant to be read over and over again, especially at bedtime.

Key: Personal Value: Bedtime

✦ **Setting and Materials Needed:** The setting is no surprise. The book sharing should take place at bedtime. The first time it is read you need to make sure the moon can be seen from one of the windows. No materials are needed.

✦ **Before Reading Activity:** Go with your child as he or she walks to the bedroom. As you pass different objects say goodnight to them. For example, you might say goodnight to the stairs, hallway, a stuffed animal, and so forth. Ask your child if there is something he or she would like to say goodnight to. Give your child the opportunity to say his or her goodnights. Before your child gets in bed, show him or her the book, *Goodnight Moon*. Say, "That's who we forgot to say goodnight to." Find a window facing the moon and say together, "Goodnight moon," then head back to bed.

✦ **During Reading Activity:**   As you read the story, just enjoy it. This is a wonderful book to read at bedtime and a wonderful book to listen to at bedtime. Make sure your child has plenty of time to examine the pictures that show the bunny's complete bedroom.

✦ **After Reading Activity:**   When you finish reading the story, ask, "What are you going to say goodnight to tomorrow when you go to bed?" If necessary give some suggestions yourself. Then read the book a second time, close the book, give your child a kiss or hug and softly say, "Goodnight."

✦ **Poetry Partners:**   "Night," "The Universe," "Birch Trees," "The Moon's the North Wind's Cooky," "The Star," "The Night is a Big, Black Car," and "Night Comes . . . " in *The Random House Book of Poetry for Children.*

✦ **Related Books:**   *Happy Birthday Moon* by Frank Asch; *Can't You Sleep Little Bear?* by Martin Waddell; *A Bedtime Book* by Joan W. Anglund; *Goodnight Gorilla* by Peggy Rathmann; *The Runaway Bunny* by Margaret Wise Brown; and *The Moon Book* by Gail Gibbons.

Book Share 5

A room without books is like a body without a soul.
   —Cicero

Title: *A Was Once an Apple Pie*

Author: Edward Lear

Illustrator: Julie Lacome

Publisher: Candlewick

Summary: This book encourages children to play with the sounds of their language as the letters A to Z are introduced in a rhythmical and non-sensical way: "A was once an apple pie, Pidy Widy Tidy Pidy Nice insidy Apple pie." Each letter follows the same predictable pattern.

Key: Phonemic Awareness, Alphabet, and Predictable and Pattern

✦ **Setting and Materials Needed:** Any comfortable setting will do. You will need pictures of interesting objects. These may be from magazines, games, photographs, or anything you have.

✦ **Before Reading Activity:** Tell your child that you are going to read him or her a silly alphabet book by an author who wrote many silly stories.

✦ **During Reading Activity:** Begin reading the book. After you have read through several letters (perhaps, A to E), read the first part of the next page and ask your child to make up nonsense rhymes that fit the pattern. For example, read "F was once a little fish, Fishy [pause]" and ask "What rhymes with fishy? How about dishy? mishy?" Encourage your child to contribute! Then read what the author wrote. Continue to read a few more pages, then stop again and ask your child for some rhymes. The more you involve your child the better, but only do this as often as your child finds it interesting.

✦ **After Reading Activity:** After reading, show your child the pictures you found and start making up silly rhymes to go with the pictures. "Look, I have a picture of a car. Listen: carsy, marsy, parsy, carsy." Ask your child to make up nonsense rhymes for the other pictures you found. If your child is finding this activity a lot of fun, leave the pictures and march around the house, pointing to things to make nonsense rhymes for: "doorsy, poorsy, boorsy, choorsy." If you can, include the letter: "Let's do our bed: B was once a little bed. Beddy, neddy, leddy, beddy. Let's climb in the little beddy." Conclude the adventure by stating that you and your child could probably write your own book!

✦ **Poetry Partners:** "Dance to your Daddie" and "A Counting-Out Rhyme" in *The Real Mother Goose;* "Alphabet Stew," "Four Seasons," "Fishes' Evening Song," "The Pizza," and "Rhyme" in *The Random House Book of Poetry for Children.*

✦ **Related Books:** Also by Edward Lear: *The Owl and the Pussycat, The Quangle Wangle's Hat, A Book of Nonsense, Daffy Down Dillies: Silly Limericks, How Pleasant to Know Mr. Lear: Nonsense Poems,* and *The Pelican Chorus and Other Nonsense.*

Book Share 6

Reading books is good,
Rereading good books is better.
　　　—Lawrence Clark Powell

Title: *Chicka Chicka Boom Boom*

Authors: Bill Martin, Jr. and John Archambault

Illustrator: Lois Ehlert

Publisher: Simon and Schuster

Summary: *Chicka Chicka Boom Boom* is an alphabet book that begins, "**A** told **B** and **B** told **C,** "I'll meet you at the top of the coconut tree." The book continues in a rhyming, singing mode with the refrain "Chicka chicka boom boom!" heard throughout. The illustrations are bold and appealing to kids. Children enjoy the story line, especially when the letters of the alphabet fall out of the coconut tree. This is a wonderful book for helping children become familiar with the alphabet letter names. It is a book you will want to read over and over.

Key: Alphabet

✦ **Setting and Materials Needed:** The book sharing can take place in any comfortable setting. You will need a pad of plain paper and some crayons.

✦ **Before Reading Activity:** Say, "I'm going to read you a book about alphabet letters getting into trouble. It is called *Chicka Chicka Boom Boom.*" Then open the book to the inside cover and show your child all the colorful letters. Say, "Look, they have each letter twice, once big and once small. Let's see if I can find the letter that starts your name." Then help your child find the letter that starts his or her name. Finally, say, "Remember, I said this book was about the letters of the alphabet getting into trouble? Let's see what trouble they get into."

✦ **During Reading Activity:** Read the story to your child and simply enjoy what it has to say. Then read it again, and this time put you finger on each large colorful letter of the alphabet as you read the story. For example, when you read the book and say, "**A** told **B**, and **B** told **C**, 'I'll meet you at the top of the coconut tree,'" point to each of the large, colorful letters at the bottom of the page as you say the letter in the story. If your child feels comfortable with the process, read the story a third time and have your child point to the large letters on each page as you say the letters in the alphabet.

✦ **After Reading Activity:** Say to your child, "Let's make our own tree to put the letters in. What kind of tree should it be? An apple tree? An orange tree?" Draw the tree on a blank sheet of paper and then look at *Chicka Chicka Boom Boom*. As you examine each letter in the story, write the letter in your child's tree (or, if your child can and would like to, have him or her write the letters). When you are finished put at the bottom of the page "An Alphabet Tree by (your child's name)." Make sure the tree is shared with lots of important and appreciative people.

✦ **Poetry Partners:** "Pat-a-Cake," "Just Like Me," "A B C," "One, Two, Three," "The Alphabet," "Pancake Day," and "Oh, Dear!" in *The Real Mother Goose*.

✦ **Related Books:** *Listen to the Rain, Up and Down on the Merry-go-Round,* and *Barn Dance* all by Bill Martin, Jr. and John Archambault; also, *The Giving Tree* by Shel Silverstein; *Alphabatics* by Suse MacDonald; and *The Alphabet Tree* by Leo Lionni.

Book Share 7

The book should be a ball of light in one's hand.
—Ezra Pound

Title: *One Zillion Valentines*

Author: Frank Modell

Publisher: William Morrow

Summary: In this delightful Valentine's Day book, Milton bemoans the fact that he never receives a valentine. Marvin informs him that he must send valentines in order to receive them. And so, the two friends decide to make one zillion valentines to distribute throughout their neighborhood. They gather colored paper, colored pencils, crayons, paints, and scissors and make valentine cards with big hearts and little hearts, skinny hearts and fat hearts, polka dot hearts and striped hearts. They deliver the valentines and sell those that are left over. With the money they earn, Marvin buys Milton a box of chocolates, and the two friends celebrate Valentine's Day together.

Key: Personal Value: Valentine's Day

✦ **Setting and Materials Needed:** Read this book in a setting with a large, available working surface. A kitchen table would be ideal. You will need supplies for making valentine cards, such as colored pencils, crayons, paints, scissors, and colored or white paper.

✦ **Before Reading Activity:** Read this book several days before Valentine's Day. Tell your child that soon it will be Valentine's Day and that you wish to read a book about two friends who celebrate Valentine's Day together. Look at the cover of the book and read the title. Ask your child where he or she thinks the one zillion valentines come from. Then say, "Let's find out!"

✦ **During Reading Activity:** Enjoy reading the book together.

✦ **After Reading Activity:**   After reading, suggest that you and your child make valentines for your family, friends, and neighbors. Show your child the supplies you have gathered and ask if there is anything else you might need. Then sit down together and begin. You may wish to return to the page in the story that shows the many hearts that Marvin and Milton drew. The childlike illustrations of hearts may spark your child's creativity. Write "Happy Valentine's Day" on the back or inside of as many of the cards as you wish. If your child would like to write the letters, let him or her! You may write the words once and let your child copy, or you may spell the words to your child as he or she writes. If your child wants you do to the writing, do so—but name the letters as you write them and then read the message to your child when you have completed it. Deliver the cards when you are able!

✦ **Poetry Partners:**   "Valentine," "I Love you," "Somebody," "Question," "Love," and "Huckleberry, Gooseberry, Raspberry Pie" in *The Random House Book of Poetry for Children; "Love" in Where the Sidewalk Ends.*

✦ **Related Books:**   *Louanne the Pig in the Mysterious Valentine* by Nancy Carlson; *Little Mouse's Big Valentine* by Thacher Hurd; *My Very Own Valentine's Day: A Book of Cooking and Crafts* by Robin West; *Four Valentines in a Rainstorm* by Felicia Bond; *One Very Best Valentine's Day* by Joan W. Blos; *The Valentine Bears* by Eve Bunting.

Book Share 8

No book that will not improve by repeated readings deserved to be read at all.
—Thomas Caryle

Title: *Is Your Mama a Llama?*

Author: Deborah Guarino

Illustrator: Steven Kellogg

Publisher: Scholastic

Summary: In this book of riddles and rhyme, a young llama asks a variety of animals, one after the other, if their mamas are llamas. Each one replies with physical or behavioral descriptions of its mama and concludes that its mama could not be a llama. When the reader turns the page, the identity of the mother is revealed. The rhythm and rhyming pattern of this book, along with its simple thesis, make it a wonderful choice for reading again and again.

Key: Phonemic Awareness

✦ **Setting and Materials Needed:** Any comfortable setting will do. A box of animal crackers is needed for the before reading activity.

✦ **Before Reading Activity:** Ask your child to name as many animals as he or she can think of. You might prompt him or her by providing settings, such as "farm," "zoo," and "jungle." Then give him or her a box of animal crackers. Look at the crackers together. Identify and sort the animals by kind. Put all the lions together. Put all the tigers together, and so forth. Let your child eat the crackers while you read the book.

✦ **During Reading Activity:** Read the book without interruption to enjoy its rhythm and rhyme.

✦ **After Reading Activity:** Read the story several times so your child is very familiar with it. Discuss with your child that the author provides two ways for readers to predict the identity of each mother in the story. The first way is the descriptions. Go back to the story and read just the descriptions of the animals and ask your child to guess the animal: "She hangs by her feet, and she lives in a cave. I do not believe that's how llamas behave." What animal is this? (bat) Then point out that the other way the author helps us to predict which animal is next is by using rhyming words. Go back again to the story and this time read only the rhyming clue for your child: "'Oh,' I said. 'You don't need to go on. I think that your mama must be a . . .'" (swan) It is important that your child be quite familiar with the book so that identifying the animals through rhyme is a successful activity.

✦ **Poetry Partners:** "All Things Bright and Beautiful," "Seal," "The Performing Seal," "The Bat," "Hurt No Living Thing," and "On Mother's Day" in *The Random House Book of Poetry for Children*; "Hush-a-bye" in *The Real Mother Goose*.

✦ **Related Books:** *Whose Baby am I? (Animals Q & A)* by Shirley Greenway; *I Love You as Much* by Laura Krauss Melmed; *Are You My Mother?* by P. D. Eastman; *Koala Lou* by Mem Fox; *If You Were My Bunny* by Kate McMullan; and *Guess How Much I Love You* by Sam McBratney.

Book Share 9

These are not books, lumps of lifeless paper,
but minds alive on the shelves.
　　　—Gilbert Highet

Title: *Cloudy with a Chance of Meatballs*

Author: Judi Barrett

Illustrator: Ron Barrett

Publisher: Atheneum (An Aladdin Book)

Summary: A grandfather tells his grandchildren the best tall-tale bedtime story ever. He spins a tale about a small community called Chewandswallow. In the town, all food comes from the sky. Instead of rain and snow falling from the sky, juice and mashed potatoes pour down. Unfortunately, the weather takes a turn for the worse. A tomato tornado, gigantic pancakes, and a heavy pea soup fog all become unwelcome additions to the Chewandswallow menu. The people have to leave Chewandswallow and settle in a new land where they get their food in supermarkets. This is a book you will want to read over and over, especially when the weather is blustery.

Key: Personal Value: Food

◆ **Setting and Materials Needed:** The book sharing should take place at the kitchen or dining room table. A piece of paper or notepad and a pencil will be needed.

◆ **Before Reading Activity:** Take your child to the refrigerator and open the door. Indicate your favorite food and ask your child to name what he or she likes best. Then ask your child where he or she thinks the preferred food comes from. (The response will probably be the grocery store, supermarket, or the name of a local store.) Tell your child, "I'm going to read you a book where food doesn't come from the store. It all comes from the sky. In this story, it rains juice, and it snows mashed potatoes." Your child might enjoy eating a snack as you read this story.

✦ **During Reading Activity:** As you read the story, make sure your child can see all the wonderful illustrations. Turn the pages slowly so that the pictures can be examined carefully and details can be noticed. There is no need for any planned discussion during reading. The pictures and content usually fully involve the listener.

✦ **After Reading Activity:** Go back through the book and look for things you and your child would like to have come from the sky. Then talk about what she or he would have for a normal noontime or evening meal. "At supper we would have a salad, some chicken, some green beans, some milk to drink, and some pudding for dessert." Tell your child you would like to have him or her help you prepare a menu for a meal. Say, "Let's pretend it comes from the sky." Write the suggested menu making sure foods are named for each part of the meal. Ask questions such as, "What drink do you want to rain from the sky?" "What do you want for vegetables?" Continue with the main course, dessert, and so on. Set a date as soon as possible for eating this meal. After the meal, again read *Cloudy with a Chance of Meatballs* as a bedtime story.

✦ **Poetry Partners:** "Jellyfish Stew," "Mabel, Remarkable Mabel," "The Flotz," "Eggs!," "No, I *Won't* Turn Orange," and "Yubbazubbies" in *The New Kid on the Block;* "I'm Hungry" in *The Random House Book of Poetry for Children.*

✦ **Related Books:** *Bread and Jam for Frances* by Russell Hoban; *Mouse Soup* and *The Popcorn Book* by Tomie dePaola; *The Wolf's Chicken Stew* by Keiko Kasza. *Animals Should Definitely* Not *Wear Clothing* and *Animals Should Definitely* Not *Act Like People* are additional books by Ron Barrett.

Book Share 10

A library is not a luxury, but one of the necessities of life.
　　—Henry Ward Beecher

Title: *Bearsie Bear and the Surprise Sleepover*

Author: Bernard Waber

Publisher: Houghton Mifflin

Summary: Bearsie Bear was just about to fall asleep one cold winter night when Moosie Moose shows up at the door and asks to sleep over. Bearsie Bear invites the moose in ("just this once") and the two jump into bed together. Moments later Cowsie Cow knocks at the door. The cow, too, asks to sleep over. The cow settles into bed and good nights are said just as Piggie Pig shows up. In this humorous story, one animal after the other comes to Bearsie Bear's home to get out of the cold. Finally, Porkie Porcupine jumps into the crowded bed for an expected result. Eventually everyone settles in for a happy sleepover.

Key: Phonemic Awareness

✦ **Setting and Materials Needed:** Any comfortable setting will do, but this story will be most fun if read as a bedtime story while snuggled in bed.

✦ **Before Reading Activity:** Look at the cover of the book with your child and read the title. Ask your child who he or she thinks is sleeping over. Open the book to the title page and read the title again. Point to the picture on the title page and ask your child how he or she thinks the bear feels about all these animals showing up at his house. Comment on the name of the bear, "Bearsie Bear," and giggle about the name together. Wonder aloud if the other animals you see in the picture have equally silly names.

✦ **During Reading Activity:** Enjoy the playful story and the playful language in this story. Notice how each of the animals has a silly name. Stop after two animals (Moosie Moose and Cowsie Cow) have joined the bear in bed and look back at the cover page. What other animals will be joining Bearsie Bear? Predict together what their names are. Continue reading until Porkie Porcupine comes to the door and each of the animals in bed says "Uh-oh." Ask your child why he or she supposes each of the animals reacts this way. Continue reading to the end of the story.

✦ **After Reading Activity:**   Look at the cover of the book where the animals are shown in the bed. Name with your child each of the animals. ("Here is the bear. Which animal is this?" and so on.) Then, tell your child that you are going to say just a little bit of each animal's name and your child is to guess which animal you are thinking about. Say the first sound (not letter!) of each of the animal's names. For instance, for fox, you will say /f/ (the sound, not the letter name). Your child should look at the animals on the cover and say "fox!" or "Foxie Fox!" If he or she has difficulty, provide more of the name to help, /f/-/o/." Try doing this with each of the animals. Notice that when you say /p/, your child may respond with either "porcupine" or "pig." Then, if your child wishes, he or she may try giving the first part of the name and letting you guess which animal he or she is thinking of. End your read-aloud time with, "And now it's time for my little boysie boy or girlsie girl to go to sleep and for Mommsie Mom or Daddsie Dad to say goodsie nightsie!"

✦ **Poetry Partners:**   "Grandpa Bear's Lullaby," "Dogs and Cats and Bears and Bats," "From: The Bed Book," and "Keep a Poem in Your Pocket" in *The Random House Book of Poetry for Children*; "Wee Willie Winkie," "Diddle Diddle Dumpling," and "The Robin" in *The Real Mother Goose.*

✦ **Related Books:**   *Henny Penny* by Paul Galdone; *Spot Sleeps Over* by Eric Hill; *The Mitten* by Jan Brett; *The Animals' Song* by David L. Harrison; *Animals in Winter* by Henrietta Bancroft and Richard G. Van Gelder; and *Funny, Funny Lyle* also by Bernard Waber.

Book Share 11

*If one cannot enjoy reading a book over and over again,
there is no use in reading at all.*
   —Oscar Wilde

Title: *Black and White Rabbit's ABC*

Author: Alan Baker

Publisher: Kingfisher

Summary: "A is for apple. B is for box, where Rabbit puts the apple." So begins this clever alphabet book in which Rabbit paints a beautiful picture of an apple, but not without several problems, such as dripping paint, spilled ink, and a paw that gets stuck in sticky-icky glue. This is a cute story that is sure to delight young readers.

Key: Alphabet

✦ **Setting and Materials Needed:** You will need watercolor paints, a paint brush, paper, an apple, other items to paint, magazines, scissors, and glue. You will want to do the activities at a table.

✦ **Before Reading Activity:** Rabbit paints a still life. You can let your child paint one, too! Put an apple on the table and ask your child to paint a picture of it. Allow your child to choose other objects to paint. He or she might want to paint several foods. Let your child find fruits, vegetables, or other foods in the refrigerator or pantry to paint. Enjoy painting and talking together. Tell your child that you want to share a book about a rabbit that paints a picture.

✦ **During Reading Activity:** Read the book. Notice that it tells a story—many alphabet books do not. Enjoy the story as you progress through the alphabet.

✦ **After Reading Activity:** Help your child label the pictures that he or she painted earlier. Do this by cutting and gluing letters from magazines underneath the pictures. (Advertisements are a good source for this activity because the letters usually are quite large.) Spell the words for your child and assist him or her in finding the letters and cutting them out. Let your child glue the letters, one at a time, onto the paper underneath the appropriate picture.

If your child is not interested in labeling his or her pictures or finds this activity too complex, use a separate piece of paper and let your child cut and glue the letters of the alphabet in order or cut out and glue letters that spell names of family members, friends, or pets. Or, he or she may enjoy simply cutting and pasting letters onto the paper randomly.

✦ **Poetry Partners:** "The Alphabet" and "ABC" in *The Real Mother Goose*; "We Heard Wally Wail" in *The New Kid on the Block*; "The Paint Box," "I'm Glad the Sky Is Painted Blue," "The Rabbit," and "Feather or Fur" in *The Random House Book of Poetry for Children*.

✦ **Related Books:** *Brown Rabbit's Shape Book, Gray Rabbit's 1, 2, 3,* and *White Rabbit's Color Book,* all by Alan Baker; *Peter Rabbit* by Beatrix Potter; *Frederick* by Leo Lionni; and *Mouse Paint* by Ellen Stoll Walsh.

Book Share 12

Reading is a basic tool in the living of a good life.
—Mortimer J. Adler

Title: *Seven Blind Mice*

Author: Ed Young

Publisher: Scholastic

Summary: This book tells the story of seven blind mice who were very surprised to find a strange Something by their pond. One by one they try to discover what this strange Something is. On successive days of the week, each mouse examines the strange Something. The strange Something is (we are giving away the surprise) an elephant, but because each blind mouse feels a different part of the elephant, each reaches a different conclusion. The seven days of the week and seven colors are introduced in this boldly illustrated book.

Key: Predictable and Pattern

✦ **Setting and Materials Needed:** The book sharing should take place at any comfortable, favorite place to read. You will need some stuffed toys or objects that are very familiar to your son or daughter. You also will need two large paper bags. In one of the bags, put your stuffed toys or objects. Close the bag so that what is inside cannot be seen.

✦ **Before Reading Activity:** Suggest that you and your child play a guessing game with a toy. Give your child a large bag and ask him or her to get a toy and slip it into the bag without you seeing it. When your child returns with the toy in the bag, close your eyes and ask your child to lift the toy out of the bag and place it in your hands. Your job is to guess what toy it is without looking at it. Feel it carefully and make comments like, "It is very soft," or "It has four legs." Think aloud as you try to identify the toy. Then, correctly if possible, guess what toy it is. Tell your child that you would like to share a book about seven blind mice who meet a strange Something by their pond. They have to determine what it is, yet they cannot see it. Ask your child to predict how the mice will accomplish this.

✦ **During Reading Activity:** Look at the cover of *Seven Blind Mice*, read the cover, and count the number of mice. Then begin reading the book. After each mouse explores the strange Something, have your child guess what he or she thinks the strange Something is. Continue until you finish the story.

✦ **After Reading Activity:** After you discuss the story, tell your child you have some things in a bag and ask if he or she would like to try to guess what they are with his or her eyes closed. Do this with two or three—or more!—objects, making positive statements when your child carefully examines the stuffed toy or familiar object.

✦ **Poetry Partners:** "It's Dark in Here," "Colors," "Joey," "Jimmy Jet and His TV Set," "Hector the Collector," "No Difference," and "Invisible Boy" in *Where the Sidewalk Ends.*

✦ **Related Books:** Two additional books by Ed Young that children enjoy are *Donkey Trouble* and *I Wish I Were a Butterfly* (illustrated by Young, written by J. Howe). Other related books include *Animals Should Definitely Not Wear Clothing* by Judi Barrett; *Seven Little Rabbits* by John Becken; *I Can Tell by Touching* by Carolyn B. Otto; and *The Mixed Up Chameleon* by Eric Carle.

Book Share 13

The first time I read an excellent book it is to me just as if I had gained a new friend; when I read over a book I have perused before, it resembles the meeting of an old one.

—Oliver Goldsmith

Title: *The Very Hungry Caterpillar*

Author: Eric Carle

Publisher: Scholastic

Summary: This is a story, not surprisingly, about a very hungry caterpillar. On Monday he eats through one apple, on Tuesday two pears, and the pattern continues through the week. The book is unique in that there are actual holes in the pages of the book where the caterpillar has eaten. At the end of the book, the hungry caterpillar changes into something very special.

Key: Predictable and Pattern

✦ **Setting and Materials Needed:** The book sharing should take place at the kitchen or dining room table. No materials will be needed.

✦ **Before Reading Activity:** Ask your child what some of his or her favorite foods are when he or she is *really* hungry. Then read the title of the story. Ask your child what he or she thinks a very hungry caterpillar might like to eat. You can make some guesses, too. Then say, "Let's read to see what the very hungry caterpillar eats in this story." We hope you and your child will follow up this Book Share experience by referring to a factual resource to discover what caterpillars really eat.

✦ **During Reading Activity:** As you read the book just enjoy the story and illustrations. Ask why there is a hole in the food on each page. Make sure your child understands that this is supposed to be where the caterpillar ate. Read the story a second time, and when you read "On Tuesday he ate through two pears, but he was still hungry," stop for a moment and count aloud the number of pears. Do this for each page.

✦ **After Reading Activity:**   Talk about all the things the caterpillar ate. Then review with your child what some of his or her favorite foods are. Then say, "Let's read the book again, but this time let's make believe that you are the caterpillar. Each day tell me what you would like to eat." Pick up the book and say, "Let's call this 'The Very Hungry (your child's name).'" Start reading the book and when you come to Monday have your child say what he or she would like to eat. Do the same thing for every page of the book. At the end of the book ask "Will you turn into a beautiful butterfly?" Tell your child he or she is beautiful already, and then talk about what he or she might be when he or she grows up.

✦ **Poetry Partners:**   "My Mouth," "Egg Thoughts," "Oodles of Noodles," "Pie Problem," "Chocolate Cake," "Eat-it-all Elaine," and "My Little Sister" in *The Random House Book of Poetry for Children*.

✦ **Related Books:**   *The Very Busy Spider, The Very Quiet Cricket, The Grouchy Ladybug, The Tiny Seed,* and *Do You Want to be My Friend?* all by Eric Carle; and *From Caterpillar to Butterfly* by Deborah Heiligman.

Book Share 14

If the crowns of all the kingdoms of the Empire were laid at my feet in exchange for my books and my love of reading, I would spurn them all.
> —Francois Fenelon

Title: *How a Seed Grows*

Author: Helene J. Jordan

Illustrator: Loretta Krupinski

Publisher: HarperCollins

Summary: This book presents a detailed, clear discussion on how seeds become plants. The author guides children through the process of planting seeds and has a clever process for helping them see how seeds grow. This is a great book for showing children that books can supply interesting, factual information. *How a Seed Grows* is part of the HarperCollins "Let's-Read-and-Find-Out Science" series.

Key: Personal Value: Gardening

◆ **Setting and Materials Needed:** The book sharing should take place outside as the weather gets springtime warm. You will need to examine the book carefully before reading it to your child. It takes quite a commitment of time and material on your part. The book details what materials you will need.

◆ **Before Reading Activity:** Show your child the cover and read the title. As you examine the cover ask, "What is the child doing?" Show your child the packet of bean seeds you purchased. Say, "This book, *How a Seed Grows*, is going to show us how to plant seeds and watch them grow."

◆ **During Reading Activity:** Read the book all the way through once. Then read it again and, with your child, follow the directions provided for planting bean seeds.

✦ **After Reading Activity:**   After you have read the book and planted the seeds, take a walk around the neighborhood and discuss all the things you see that grow from seeds. When you return from your walk, you and your child should tell important others (grandma, grandpa, younger, older brother or sister) one or two of the things you saw that grow from seeds and what you have planted that will be growing soon.

✦ **Poetry Partners:**   "Four Seasons," "Smells," "Spring Is," "Good-by My Winter Suit," "Spring," "Ode to Spring," and "Easter" in *The Random House Book of Poetry for Children.*

✦ **Related Books:**   The following are some of the other books in the Harper-Collins science series: *How Many Teeth?* by Paul Showers; *From Tadpole to Frog* by Wendy Pfeffer; *A Nest Full of Eggs* by Priscilla B. Jenkins; *I Can Tell by Touching* by Carolyn Otto; *My Hands* by Aliki; and *What's It Like to Be a Fish?* by Wendy Pfeffer. See also *From Seed to Plant* by Gail Gibbons.

Book Share 15

It had been startling and disappointing to me to find out that story books had been written by people, that books were not natural wonders, coming up of themselves like grass.

—Eudora Welty

Title: *The Carrot Seed*

Author: Ruth Krauss

Illustrator: Crockett Johnson

Publisher: Harper & Row

Summary: A classic written in 1945, *The Carrot Seed* tells of a young boy who plants a carrot seed. His parents tell him they are afraid it won't come up, and his older brother is *sure* it won't come up. The young boy is diligent in his efforts at watering and weeding and, at the conclusion of the story, a truly impressive carrot does, indeed, come up.

Key: Personal Value: Gardening

✦ **Setting and Materials Needed:** Book Share 14 suggested you and your child plant beans. This time it is carrots! You will need a packet of carrot seeds (the packet should have a picture of carrots on the outside) and a place to plant them. This can be in an outside garden or some form of container with soil in it.

✦ **Before Reading Activity:** Show your child the packet containing the carrot seeds. Ask what he or she thinks is inside. Share the seeds with your child and let him or her hold the packet while you begin reading *The Carrot Seed*.

✦ **During Reading Activity:** As you read the story, make sure the simple, yet expressive, illustrations can be seen. When the little boy waters the seed and pulls up the weeds for the second time, turn to the next page where it says,

"And then one day . . . " read the page and, before you turn to the next page, ask your child if the carrot is going to come up. If he or she is unsure, look together at the illustration and point out the movement of the ground.

✦ **After Reading Activity:**   Discuss the size of the truly impressive carrot the little boy grew and talk about whether someone could really grow a carrot that size. Ask your child if he or she would like to grow some carrots. Follow the directions on the packet. Then, each time before you water the seeds and pull up the weeds, read *The Carrot Seed*.

✦ **Poetry Partners:**   "Smells," "The Worm," "When," "Celery," "Soap," "Flowers Are a Silly Bunch," and "Rainy Nights" in *The Random House Book of Poetry for Children*.

✦ **Related Books:**   Ruth Krauss has written a number of outstanding books. The following are some that children especially enjoy: *The Happy Day; A Hole Is to Dig: A First Book of First Definitions; I'll Be You and You Be Me; My Little Library; Somebody Else's Nut Tree and Other Tales from Children;* and *A Very Special House*.

Book Share 16

A good reader is one who has imagination, memory, a dictionary, and some artistic sense.
  —Vladimir Nabokov

Title: *Alphabet City*

Author: Stephen T. Johnson

Publisher: Viking Children's Books

Summary: The idea for this book came to the author while he was walking down a city street. He noticed an ornamental keystone that looked like the letter *S*. Then he saw the letter *A* in a sawhorse and the letter *Z* in a fire escape. The book is a collection of photographs depicting the letters *A* through *Z* in public places. The author encourages children and adults to look at their world in a new way.

Key: Alphabet

✦ **Setting and Materials Needed:** The before reading activity requires you to explore your indoor and outdoor environments. During reading, find any comfortable place to share the book with your child. Paper and crayons are needed for the after reading activity.

✦ **Before Reading Activity:** This activity may take place over several days before sharing the book. Notice letters of the alphabet in the environment. In addition to obvious examples, such as letters on magazine covers, traffic signs, and billboards, try to find letter shapes in unexpected places. For example, does a wheel on a tricycle look like the letter *O*? Does a crack in the sidewalk look like the letter *N*? After you have explored your environment for letters, tell your child that the book you are about to read is called *Alphabet City*. Explain that the author saw letters in many places and took pictures of them to make this book.

✦ **During Reading Activity:** Share the book with your child. Ask him or her to find and trace the letter on each page. Some of the letters are difficult to find, so be prepared to assist. You might hold your child's index finger and guide it over the letter. You will also want to discuss what the pictures are.

✦ **After Reading Activity:** Draw pictures with your child using letters of the alphabet. For example, you might draw several *T*'s and connect them with power lines. The *T*'s become power poles. After drawing an *S*, you might add eyes to one end. Now the *S* is a snake. Look at a family photo album or magazine and see if you can find letter shapes in the pictures.

✦ **Poetry Partners:** "Alphabet Stew," "Rudolph Is Tired of the City," "Sunrise," "Concrete Mixers," "Sing a Song of People," "City," and "The City Dump" in *The Random House Book of Poetry for Children.*

✦ **Related Books:** Books about finding shapes in the world around us are *Color Farm* and *Color Zoo* by Lois Ehlert. Other city books include *Waving: A Counting Book* by Peter Sis; *The Village of Round and Square Houses* by Ann Grifalconi; *Country Mouse and City Mouse* by Patricia C. and Fredrick McKissack; and *City Seen From A to Z* by Rachel Isadora.

Book Share 17

When I see books that I have read on library shelves, it is like running into an old friend on the street. I often take a book down and browse through it, even though I have no intention of checking it out of the library and reading it once again . . . Like friends, these books have gone into the making of whatever and whoever I am.

—Kevin Starr

Title: *An Egg Is an Egg*

Author: Nicki Weiss

Publisher: The Trumpet Club

Summary: This simple rhyming book is about changes. An egg, for instance, becomes a chick. The theme that everything can change runs throughout the book until the end when the reader discovers that some things *do* stay the same: the love of a parent for a child.

Key: Personal Value: Changes and Ongoing Love

✦ **Setting and Materials Needed:** A current photograph of your child, a photograph of him or her as an infant, a piece of paper, and a writing instrument are needed.

✦ **Before Reading Activity:** Tell your child that this book is about some things that change. Look at the cover. Ask your child what he or she sees in the picture that is going to change (the egg). See if you can think of other things that change (caterpillars become butterflies; day turns into night). Look around the room or out a window and see if you can find anything that has changed.

✦ **During Reading Activity:** As you read, comment on anything that shows up in the book that you may have thought about before reading. Note how interesting it is that you and the author thought of the same idea. Then, before the end of the story, pause and say "I wonder if everything changes in this book."

✦ **After Reading Activity:** After you have finished the book, look at the two photographs of your child together. Then think about the ways your child has changed since he or she was a baby (for example, he or she has more hair, can speak, can draw, can ride a tricycle, has teeth, is taller). Write these on the left side of a paper that has been folded down the middle lengthwise. Title this half of the paper, <u>Ways I Have Changed</u>. Next, think of ways your child is the same (for example, he or she still has brown hair, brown eyes, still laughs when tickled, still likes hugs). Write these on the right side of the paper and title this list, <u>Ways I Am the Same</u>. Be sure to add to this list that he or she is still your child. Display this on the refrigerator or a bulletin board. Feel free to add to it over time.

✦ **Poetry Partners:** "Egg Thoughts," "Meg's Egg," "The Opposite of Two," "Question," and "Somebody" in *The Random House Book of Poetry for Children* and "Hug o' War" and "Love" in *Where the Sidewalk Ends.*

✦ **Related Books:** *Guess How Much I Love You* by Sam McBratney; *Koala Lou* by Mem Fox; *Horton Hatches an Egg* by Dr. Seuss; *Mama, Do You Love Me?* by Barbara M. Joosse; *The Kissing Hand* by Audrey Penn; and *Love You Forever* by Robert Munsch.

Book Share 18

The sum of it all is: read what you like, because you like it, seeing no other reason and no other profit than the experience of reading. If you enjoy the experience it is well; but whether you enjoy it or not the experience is worth having.

—Holbrook Jackson

Title: *If You Give a Mouse a Cookie*

Author: Laura Joffe Numeroff

Illustrator: Felicia Bond

Publisher: Scholastic

Summary: A boy describes what might happen if you give a mouse a cookie. He will want milk, then a straw, and the story progresses until giving a mouse a cookie becomes a very involved process. At the conclusion of the story, the boy finds himself right back where he began.

Key: Predictable and Pattern

✦ **Setting and Materials Needed:** The book sharing should take place at the kitchen or dining room table. You will need a glass of milk and a plate of chocolate chip (or any favorite) cookies—perhaps some you have just baked with your child. You also will need a copy of *If You Give a Moose a Muffin* or *If You Give a Pig a Pancake* by the same author.

✦ **Before Reading Activity:** Have the glass of milk and plate of chocolate chip cookies on the table. As you and your child begin eating the cookies and drinking the milk, ask your child if he or she would like a straw for the milk and a napkin for the cookie. Then begin reading *If You Give a Mouse a Cookie*.

✦ **During Reading Activity:** As you read the story make sure all the delightful illustrations can be seen. Stop reading when you get to the point where it is stated, "When you give him the milk, . . . " and ask, "Now I wonder what he'll want?" Accept any answer and if your child doesn't answer, think aloud what you think the mouse might like. "Let's see, you're drinking your milk with a straw. I wonder if the mouse will want a straw." Some children will want to hear the remainder of the book without making any more predictions. Other children will enjoy guessing before you turn each page what the mouse's next request will be.

✦ **After Reading Activity:**   Laugh about the story together. Then, show your child how easy it is to retell the story by looking at the pictures on each page. Encourage your child to retell the story as he or she flips through the pages. Then, look through the pages of either *If You Give a Moose a Muffin* or *If you Give a Pig a Pancake* by the same author. Can you and your child use the pictures to tell the entire story before reading it? Give it a try! Then read the author's words to see how well you did. (You may like your version better!)

Notice the titles of *If You Give a Moose a Muffin* and *If You Give Pig a Pancake*. The author used alliteration; the words *moose* and *muffin* begin with the same sound, and *pig* and *pancake* begin with the same sound. You may want to invent some more titles for this series. For example, how about a book entitled, *If You Give a Dog a Doughnut?* What if the book were about a cat? a tiger? Encourage your child to think of food items that begin with the same sound as the animal's name, but applaud any response.

✦ **Poetry Partners:**   "The House That Jack Built," "Bat, Bat," "For Baby," "Over the Water," "Caesar's Song," "Little Jack Horner," and "Pease Porridge" in *The Real Mother Goose*.

✦ **Related Books:**   *Hippos Go Berserk* by Sandra Boynton; and *If You Give a Pig a Pancake, If You Give a Moose a Muffin, The Chicken Sisters, Dogs Don't Wear Sneakers, Chimps Don't Wear Glasses,* and *Two for Stew* all by Laura J. Numeroff.

Book Share 19

The fact that a book is famous is enough to scare off some people who, if they had the courage to open the pages, would find there delight and profit. We make the mistake of fearing that the immortal things of art must be approached through special studies.
  —John Erskine

Title: *A is for Artist: A Getty Museum Alphabet*

Author: J. Paul Getty Museum

Illustrator: Various

Publisher: J. Paul Getty Museum

Summary: Details from paintings housed in the Getty Museum are used to illustrate this alphabet book. On the first page, "A is for artist," we see a portion of the Jan Steen painting entitled "The Drawing Lesson." On the second page, "B is for bumblebee," we see a close-up of a bumblebee from the Ambrosius Bosschaert the Elder painting entitled, "Flower Still Life." This book exposes young children to famous pieces of art as they learn the alphabet. On the last pages of the book is a gallery of the complete paintings.

Key: Alphabet

✦ **Setting and Materials Needed:** A visit to a local art museum or store would enhance this reading experience greatly. After reading, watercolors, oil pastels, colored chalk or pencils, or some media are required. Supply some paper, and find a comfortable table and chair for you and your child to work at together.

✦ **Before Reading Activity:** Before sharing this book with your child, take a trip to a local art museum, a university gallery, or a mall gallery. Talk about the works of art that you see, including how they make you feel. Notice the colors, textures, and details.

✦ **During Reading Activity:** Read the book. Sometimes ask your child to point to the item referred to in the text. "R is for ribbon." "Where is the ribbon?" "T is for tambourine." "Where is the tambourine?" Provide opportunities for your child to predict the text. "L is for . . . " As your child looks at the picture of lemons on a tree, he or she will probably guess "lemon!" At the bottom of each page is the name of the painting and the artist. Share this information with your child, as long as he or she is interested. At the end of the book are the complete paintings. After reading, it is fun to flip back and forth from the text to the complete paintings and try to find the item in the complete painting. Sometimes the item is a very small portion of the complete painting.

✦ **After Reading Activity:** A wonderful follow-up to this book is to have your child become an artist. Use whatever media you have available—watercolors, oil pastels, and so forth. Sit together at a table, and ask your child to pick a letter of the alphabet and tell you what it is for. Or, if more appropriate for your child, let him or her tell you what he wants to draw ("cat") and you say, "Okay! C is for cat." Write it on the bottom of the paper. Then let your child create! Do as many letters of the alphabet as your child desires, or let your child do as many "C" words as he or she desires. After the pictures dry, make a book by writing a title page that includes your child's name as "artist," staple the pages together, and share the book with others.

✦ **Poetry Partners:** "What is Red?" "What is Pink?" "What is Orange?" "Rhinos Purple, Hippos Green," and "Yellow" in *The Random House Book of Poetry for Children*; "Colors" and "Invisible Boy" in *Where the Sidewalk Ends*.

✦ **Related Books:** *The Art Lesson* by Tomie dePaola; *Mama's Perfect Present* by Diane Goode; *The Etcher's Studio* by Arthur Geisert; *Color* by Ruth Heller; *Draw Me a Star* by Eric Carle; and *Harold and the Purple Crayon* by Crockett Johnson.

Book Share 20

*The greatest fun in reading aloud lies in the adventure of
the thing—the sense of taking a child on an exploration
of a fascinating territory into which you alone have
penetrated.*

—Leonard Wibberley

Title: *What Do You Do with a Kangaroo?*

Author: Mercer Mayer

Publisher: Scholastic

Summary: This is a story about a young girl who finds a kangaroo in her
bed. It is the first of many animals she finds in such locations as the bath-
room, the bedroom, and the kitchen. Each time she finds one of the animals, she asks the question, "What do you do?" She then takes action.
What Do You Do with a Kangaroo? is a story of a young girl taking charge
until, at the end of the story, she discovers that sometimes if you can't beat
them, you probably should join them.

Key: Predictable and pattern book

✦ **Setting and Materials Needed:** The book sharing should take place at any
favorite reading location. You will need as many stuffed animals as you have
around the house for a later bedtime activity.

✦ **Before Reading Activity:** Show your child the cover of the book and read
the title. Ask your child if the girl in the picture looks happy with the kangaroo. Then say, "Let's read the story to find of if she is happy or unhappy with
the kangaroo."

✦ **During Reading Activity:** Mercer Mayer is a popular children's illustrator.
Be sure to take time to enjoy the pictures. Also, after the girl has taken action
against the kangaroo and the opossum, have your child answer the question,
"What do you do?" for animals encountered during the rest of the story (before you read what the character does). However, you may not wish to do this

with every animal, unless your child wants to, as it may get in the way of appreciating the story. At the conclusion of the story when the girl finds all of the animals in her bed and asks the question, "Now I'll say it again: *What do you do?*" ask your child what he or she would do, then read the conclusion.

✦ **After Reading Activity:**   When you have finished reading the story, talk about what a fun book it was and ask the question, "What would you do if you found your bed full of animals?" Talk about the answer in a fun and positive way. That night, put as many stuffed animals as you can find on your child's bed. Do not let your child see you do it. Then, when he or she gets ready for bed and sees the animals, say "Where did these come from and what are you going to do?" Discuss the options. Then, as your child snuggles in bed, surrounded with animals, read *What Do You Do with a Kangaroo?* again. When the story is finished, put all the animals at the foot of the bed, and wish your child sweet dreams.

✦ **Poetry Partners:**   "Alligators Are Unfriendly," "Never Mince Words with a Shark," "Oh, Teddy Bear," "Ballad of a Boneless Chicken," "Boing! Boing! Squeak!" "Today Is a Day to Crow About," and "I'm Bold, I'm Brave" in *The New Kid on the Block.*

✦ **Related Books:**   The following are all great books by Mercer Mayer: *Just for You, There's a Nightmare in My Closet, There's an Alligator under My Bed,* and *A Boy, a Dog, and a Frog* (wordless book). In addition, he has written several *Just Me and . . .* books that include *Just Me and My Dad, Just Me and My Mom,* and others such as cousin, puppy, babysitter, and little brother.

Book Share 21

The reading which has pleased, will please when repeated ten times.

—Horace

Title: *Corduroy*

Author: Don Freeman

Publisher: Viking

Summary: Corduroy is a stuffed bear in a department store who longs for someone to buy him. One day a young shopper notices Corduroy. She asks her mother if she may buy him, but her mother says no; they have spent too much money already. Her mother also points out that the bear is missing a button on his overalls. Corduroy is surprised to learn this, and that night, after the store has closed, he decides to search the store for his button. In his search, he makes so much noise that the night guard discovers him and puts him back on his shelf, with his mission unaccomplished. The next morning the girl returns, having emptied her piggy bank, to buy Corduroy. She takes him home and, although she likes him just the way he is, she sews a new button on his overalls to make him more comfortable. Corduroy is very happy to have a home.

Key: Personal Value: Stuffed Animals

✦ **Setting and Materials Needed:** You will need stuffed animals and supplies (such as a needle and thread and scissors) for repairing them.

✦ **Before Reading Activity:** Tell your child that you are going to read a book about a stuffed animal and that before you begin you and your child should gather together your child's favorite stuffed animals. As you gather them, talk about the animals and reminisce about where and when your child obtained them. ("Here's your green bunny! Remember when Grandma gave it to you for Easter?") Tell your child that the book you are about to read is about a child and her teddy bear.

✦ **During Reading Activity:** Enjoy reading the book.

✦ **After Reading Activity:**   Comment that Corduroy needed a new button sewn on. Ask your child to examine his or her animals to determine if they need repair. Perform any repairs you are able to do. Be sure to have your child assist in any reasonable way so that he or she feels a part of the process. If no repairs are needed, you might want to do something creative to enhance the appearance of an animal. Would any of them look good with buttons? How about putting a scarf or kerchief around the neck of one of the animals?

✦ **Poetry Partners:**   "Wendy in Winter," "Together," "From: A Christmas Package," and "The Opposite of Two" in *The Random House Book of Poetry for Children*; "Oh, Teddy Bear" in *The New Kid on the Block*; "Hector the Collector" in *Where the Sidewalk Ends*; "Buttons" in *The Real Mother Goose*.

✦ **Related Books:**   *A Pocket for Corduroy* by Don Freeman; *When the Teddy Bears Came* and *Let's Go Home, Little Bear* both by Martin Waddell; *Jesse Bear, What Will You Wear?* by Nancy White Carlstrom; *The Bear* by Raymond Briggs; *Bears* by Helen Gilks.

Book Share 22

Books are not made for furniture, but there is nothing else that so beautifully furnishes a house.
—Henry Ward Beecher

Title: *Stone Soup*

Author: Ann McGovern

Illustrator: Nola Langer

Publisher: Scholastic

Summary: A young man comes to a village hungry and tired. He goes up to a house and asks a lady for food. She tells him she has nothing to give him. He tells her he doesn't need anything but a stone, that he can make soup from a stone. The lady puts the stone in a pot of water and starts boiling the water. The young man tells her it will boil faster if she just adds some onions. This happens over and over, with new items being added, until the woman has made a delicious soup. They eat the soup. The young man then leaves, taking the soup with him, and says, "What a fine supper I will have tomorrow."

Key: Predictable and Pattern

✦ **Setting and Materials Needed:** The book sharing should take place at the kitchen or dining room table. You will be eating your child's favorite soup during this activity so you will need a can or container of this soup. You will also need a clean rock about the size of a fifty-cent piece.

✦ **Before Reading Activity:** This activity would take place best over the noon meal. As you heat your child's favorite soup read or discuss the ingredients. You might say, "Listen, this soup has some great things in it. It has chicken and carrots—and no wonder it tastes so good." Once the soup is heated, serve it and say, "I'm going to read you a book called *Stone Soup*. I wonder how soup can be made from a stone."

✦ **During Reading Activity:**   As you read the story and eat your soup, make a slight pause each time a new ingredient is added to the soup the lady is making. For example, when the lady says, "This soup looks good" and the young man says, "It would look better if you threw in a . . . " pause for a moment just before ". . . a chicken or two." Also each time the lady says, "Soup from a stone, fancy that," pause briefly. This gives your child the opportunity to say mentally the refrain right along with you.

✦ **After Reading Activity:**   The next day, or as soon as possible, place your clean stone outside your house in a location easily found. Read *Stone Soup* again and ask your child if he or she would like to make some stone soup for the evening meal. Say, "Let's go outside and see if we can find a good stone." Once the stone is located, wash it, and then follow the directions for stone soup in the book. That evening, serve the soup and read the book to the whole family. Be sure to discuss your son or daughter's role in the stone-soup-making process.

✦ **Poetry Partners:**   "I Must Remember," "Pancake?" "Sleeping Sardines," "Ridiculous Rose," "Peanut-butter Sandwich," "Lazy Jane," and "Recipe for a Hippopotamus Sandwich" in *Where the Sidewalk Ends.*

✦ **Related Books:**   *Mouse Soup* by Arnold Lobel; three different *Stone Soup* books by Marcia Brown, Tony Ross, and John Stewig. Other favorite books by Ann McGovern are *The Lady in the Box* and *Too Much Noise.*

Book Share 23

I am sure I read every book of fairy tales in our branch library, with but one complaint—all that golden hair. Never mind—my short brown hair became long and golden as I read and when I grew up I would write a book about a brown-haired girl to even things up.

—Beverly Cleary

Title: *Christina Katerina & the Box*

Author: Patricia Lee Gauch

Illustrator: Doris Burn

Publisher: Coward, McCann & Geoghegan

Summary: Christina Katerina loves boxes, so one day when a refrigerator is delivered to her home, she quickly claims the box and drags it to the front yard. There, her imagination takes over, and over the course of several days, the box becomes a castle, a clubhouse, a racing car, and a ballroom. After much wear and tear on the box, she finally lets her mother deposit it in the trash. She doesn't mind too much, though, because her good friend Fats Watson has new washer and drier boxes, and the fun can start all over again!

Key: Personal Value: Imagination

✦ **Setting and Materials Needed:** A large box or two are a must for this activity. You also will need crayons, or markers, scissors, and your imagination!

✦ **Before Reading Activity:** Show your child the box(es). Talk about what boxes are used for—packing things to move them, storing things. Then tell your child that boxes are also for having fun. Young children love boxes, often more than the toys that come in them, so be playful. Put your child inside the box, and pretend it's a car. Zoom your child around the house (always a favorite activity of our children)! If it is large enough, turn it on its side, and pretend it's a cave. Crawl inside. Have fun playing with the box for awhile.

✦ **During Reading Activity:** Read the book. After Christina uses the box for a castle, and then a clubhouse, ask your child if he or she thinks that Christina is ready to throw away the box yet. Read on to find out what Christina does next. Once the racing car is damaged, ask your child again if he or she thinks Christina is ready to throw away the box. Be surprised to discover that Christina still has a use for the box. Ask your child what he or she thinks Christina and Fats will do with the washer and drier boxes.

✦ **After Reading Activity:** Now look at your box (or boxes) again. Talk to your child about what you can do with it. Perhaps you would like to use it as a car again. Decorate the car. Draw a door on two sides. Perhaps you and your child would like to cut down the sides and create a ballroom, as Christina did. What other ideas do you have?

✦ **Poetry Partners:** "Two Boxes," "Ickle Me, Pickle Me, Tickle Me Too," "Homemade Boat," "Sidewalk," and "Invention" from *Where the Sidewalk Ends;* "Michael Built a Bicycle" from *The New Kid on the Block;* and "Tired Tim" from *The Random House Book of Poetry for Children.*

✦ **Related Books:** Other books by the author include *Christina Katerina and the Time She Quit the Family; Bravo, Tanya;* and *Dance, Tanya.* Related books that your child might enjoy are *Harold and the Purple Crayon* by Crockett Johnson; *What Can You Do With A Shoe?* by Beatrice Schenk DeRegniers; and *Josephine's 'Magination* by Arnold Jack Dobrin.

Book Share 24

*Blessed be the inventor of the alphabet, pen and printing
press! Life would be—to me in all events—a terrible
thing without books.*
  —L. M. Montgomery

Title: *Tikki Tikki Tembo*

Retold by: Arlene Mosel

Illustrator: Blair Lent

Publisher: Henry Holt

Summary: Tikki Tikki Tembo No Sa Rembo Chari Bari Ruchi Pip Peri
Pembo is a Chinese boy whose mother gave him this great long name because he is the first-born son in the family. His younger brother, considered
less important, is named Chang. One day Tikki Tikki Tembo falls into a
well. His brother runs down the hill to tell their mother of his brother's
plight. It takes much energy and breath to say his brother's name with the
reverence that his mother demands and to explain his predicament. When
his mother understands, she sends him to fetch the old man with the ladder. Chang takes much time explaining the situation to the old man with
the ladder. The delay caused by having to say Tikki Tikki Tembo's long
name almost costs Tikki Tikki Tembo his life. It is for this reason that the
Chinese now give all their children short names, according to this legend.

Key: Personal value: Names

◆ **Setting and Materials Needed:**   Any comfortable setting will do. You will
need sidewalk chalk for the after reading activity.

◆ **Before Reading Activity:**   Discuss with your child the history of his or her
name—how it was selected and why it is special. Also discuss the names of sib-
lings and any family traditions related to naming children. Explain that Tikki
Tikki Tembo is a Chinese legend about a boy whose very special name causes a
serious problem.

✦ **During Reading Activity:**   Throughout the reading of this book, encourage your child to participate by attempting to say the names of the two children.

✦ **After Reading Activity:**   After reading this book, you and your child will have fun listing long names and short names. Think of family and friends who have long and short names. Write them in chalk on your patio and compare the length of the names.

✦ **Poetry Partners:**   "My Name Is ..." and "Too Many Daves" in *The Random House Book of Poetry for Children*; "If I Had a Brontosaurus," "Sarah Cynthia Sylvia Stout Would Not Take the Garbage Out," "Ickle Me, Pickle Me, Tickle Me Too," and "Fred" in *Where the Sidewalk Ends*; "Elizabeth" in *The Real Mother Goose*.

✦ **Related Books:**   Books about names include *Chrysanthemum* by Kevin Henkes; *A Dinosaur Named After Me* by Bernard Most; *Mommy Doesn't Know My Name* by Suzanne Williams; and *A My Name Is Alice* by Jane Bayer. Two enjoyable Chinese tales are *The Crane Girl* by Veronika Martenova Charles and *The Empty Pot* by Demi.

Book Share 25

And how I felt it beat
under my pillow, in the morning dark,
An hour before the sun would let me read!
My books!
—William Hazlitt

Title: *In the Small, Small Pond*

Author: Denise Fleming

Publisher: Henry Holt

Summary: "In the small, small pond . . . wiggle, jiggle, tadpoles wriggle . . . " So begins this delightful book about life in a pond. Geese parade, herons plunge, minnows scatter. This beautifully illustrated book provides an excellent opportunity for talking about animals in a pond environment.

Key: Personal Value: Nature

✦ **Setting and Materials Needed:** This book is best read by a pond. Your local park may have a pond or lake that you can enjoy. Take your child to visit it, and bring the book with you.

✦ **Before Reading Activity:** Walk beside the lake or pond and look for living creatures that inhabit it. You may see fish, ducks, frogs, turtles, mosquitoes, and other creatures. Let your child point out any animals he or she sees. What are they? You may need to provide the labels for the animals. ("What do you see? Do you know what that is called? It is a heron.") Then ask your child to describe what the animals are doing—swimming, diving, sitting. Talk about the animals.

✦ **During Reading Activity:** Read the book next to the pond, with your child on your lap. Your child may interrupt you to say, "We saw tadpoles!" or you may want to ask, "Did we see any minnows? Let's look again." It is okay to interrupt the reading of this book to explore again, but don't do it too often. Settle down and enjoy the illustrations and the language the author uses to describe what the animals are doing.

✦ **After Reading Activity:**   After reading the story, you and your child can act out the movements of some of the animals described in the book, or others that you see at the pond. Waddle and wade like the geese. Circle and swirl like the whirligigs. Click and clack your "claws." Ask your child if there are any animals he or she would add to the book. Is there anything you saw that the author omitted? What would you have that animal do? Finally, surprise your child with a bag of old bread, and feed the ducks.

✦ **Poetry Partners:**   "The YipiYuk" and "The Silver Fish" in *Where the Sidewalk Ends*; "On the Bridge," "Fishes' Evening Song," "The Muddy Puddle," "Daddy Fell into the Pond," and "Did You Ever Go Fishing?" in *The Random House Book of Poetry for Children*.

✦ **Related Books:**   Other books by Denise Fleming include *Barnyard Banter; In the Tall, Tall Grass; Lunch;* and *Count!* See also *Box Turtle at Long Pond* by William T. George and *The Pig in the Pond* by Martin Waddell.

Book Share 26

*As a child I felt that books were holy objects, to be
caressed, rapturously sniffed, and devotedly provided
for. I gave my life up to them—and I still do. I continue
to do what I did as a child: dream of books, make books,
and collect books.*
  —Maurice Sendak

Title: *The Icky Bug Alphabet Book*

Author: Jerry Pallotta

Illustrator: Ralph Masiello

Publisher: Charlesbridge

Summary: Author Jerry Pallotta provides fascinating information about
a variety of insects, arachnids, and spiders—one for each letter of the alphabet—in this nicely illustrated alphabet book. Your child will enjoy
learning about the little creatures as he or she progresses through the letters of the alphabet.

Key: Alphabet

◆ **Setting and Materials Needed:** This is a fun book to read outdoors. You
will need a magnifying glass for the before reading activity. Magazines, newspapers, or wrapping paper with letters of the alphabet on it, crayons or marking pens, and scissors are needed for the after reading activity.

◆ **Before Reading Activity:** Before you read this book, talk with your child
about the bugs you have seen on your street, in your yard, or in your house.
Most children are familiar with ants, crickets, and lady bugs, to name a few,
and are eager to talk about them. Try to locate a few of these little creatures
and look at them through the magnifying glass. Notice how many body parts
they have. Count their legs. Watch them move. Appreciate the diversity of
nature.

✦ **During Reading Activity:**   Settle down into a comfortable position on your lawn, your porch, or in your home. Tell your child you are going to read an alphabet book about bugs. Read the book. Encourage your child to comment on any of the creatures he or she sees on the pages of the book.

✦ **After Reading Activity:**   Ask your child which animals he or she liked. Go back to those pages and enjoy them again. Move to a table or area with a flat surface. Look at the book and point out how the author moves from one letter to the next, A to Z, to write his book. Ask your child if he or she would like to go on a hunt for letters. Which letters would he or she like to find? Give your child a crayon or marking pen and ask him or her to circle the selected letters on the printed materials you provide. Magazines and newspapers are acceptable, especially if you direct your child's attention to the headlines and larger print. Many wrapping papers have the letters of the alphabet sprinkled across them and provide a fun source of print. Based on your child's choices, assist him or her in finding the letters. Circle them.

✦ **Poetry Partners:**   "Hurt No Living Thing," "Green Stems," "Praying Mantis," "Crickets," "A Bug Sat in a Silver Flower," "The Bug," and "Hey, Bug!" in *The Random House Book of Poetry for Children*.

✦ **Related Books:**   Other alphabet books by Jerry Pallotta include *The Bird Alphabet Book, The Ocean Alphabet Book, The Flower Alphabet Book, The Yucky Reptile Alphabet Book, The Frog Alphabet Book, The Furry Alphabet Book, The Dinosaur Alphabet Book, The Underwater Alphabet Book,* and *The Victory Garden Alphabet Book*. The author also has a collection of counting books, including *The Icky Bug Counting Book*.

Book Share 27

I recall reading with such intensity that my mother forbade me to go to the 82nd Street library because I was so inflamed with fairy stories I couldn't sleep.
—Richard Stern

Title: *Cock-a-Doodle-Moo!*

Author: Bernard Most

Publisher: Harcourt Brace

Summary: A rooster discovers that it has lost its voice one morning and is unable to awaken everyone on the farm. Learning of the problem, a cow attempts to help but can't say "cock-a-doodle-doo" quite right. The resulting wake-up calls (mock-a-moodle moo, sock-a-noodle-roo, and so on) give everyone an early morning laugh. This book is a natural for developing a child's awareness of sounds.

Key: Phonemic Awareness

✦ **Setting and Materials Needed:** Plastic farm animals and even a play farm house could be used but are not necessary. No special setting is needed.

✦ **Before Reading Activity:** Go outdoors for a few moments and listen for both natural and man-made sounds. Pay particular attention to animal sounds. Do you hear birds? frogs? crickets? dogs? other animals? Talk about the sounds that different animals make and imitate those sounds with your child.

Read the title of the book. Ask your child what animal makes a sound almost like the title of the book (a rooster). Ponder together why the title has the "moo" instead of the "doo" in the rooster's cry.

✦ **During Reading Activity:** At the onset of this story, each sleeping animal makes its traditional sound with a "z-z-z" added to the beginning. Your child will hear "z-z-zcheep" from the chicks, "z-z-zcluck" from the hen, "z-z-zoink" from the pigs, and "z-z-zmoo" from the cows. After page 7, stop and ask your child to predict what sound the sleeping ducks will make.

After page 11, ask your child how he or she would solve the rooster's problem. If the rooster cannot use its voice, how might it awaken the farmer and his animals? Be accepting and encouraging of all possibilities.

✦ **After Reading Activity:**   Ask why the animals laughed when they were awakened.

Say "cock-a-doodle-doo" in as many different funny ways as the two of you can think of.

Use any toys you have to reenact the story. Gather farm animals and a farm house and make noises with your child!

✦ **Poetry Partners:**   "On the Ning Nang Nong," "The Cow," and "To Be or Not to Be" in *The Random House Book of Poetry for Children;* "Cock-a-Doodle-Do!" "The Black Hen," "The Flying Pig," and "Cock Crow" in *The Real Mother Goose.*

✦ **Related Books:**   *Rooster Crows* by Ragnhild Scamell; *Cock-A-Doodle Dudley* by Bill Peet; *The Cow That Went Oink* by Bernard Most; *Too Much Noise* by Ann Mc-Govern; *Baby Animals* by Harry McNaught; *Who Said Moo?* by Harriet Ziefert and Simms Taback.

Book Share 28

Reading is to the mind what exercise is to the body.
— Sir Richard Steele

Title: *Everybody Needs a Rock*

Author: Byrd Baylor

Illustrator: Peter Parnall

Publisher: Aladdin

Summary: In this beautiful, poetic, yet down-to-earth book, a child describes ten rules for selecting your own personal rock.

Key: Personal Value: Rocks

✦ **Setting and Materials Needed:** Read this story in any comfortable place. Be sure to read during daylight hours so that you can go outside to find a rock.

✦ **Before Reading Activity:** Read the title of the book to your child and ask what he or she thinks it is about. Why would everyone need a rock? Does your child like rocks? Can you recall together times that you have played with rocks? Do you have any special rocks in your home? Look at the front cover of the book and point to the rock in the girl's hand.

✦ **During Reading Activity:** Enjoy reading the story uninterrupted. Many children find it unusual and fascinating.

✦ **After Reading Activity:** Go outdoors with your child and each of you, following the rules outlined, find a rock! Although the book says that you do not need to tell anyone what is special about your rock, you will probably enjoy sharing your rock and your reasons for selecting it with your child. Your child is likely to do the same.

Together hold your rocks under water to see how they look. Slip them into pockets to see how they fit. Toss them in the air to see how they feel when you catch them.

If your child shows an interest, you may wish to write a list of the qualities of each of your rocks. Model the process by describing a few qualities of your rock and then recording them on a piece of paper. For example, (1) It is round. (2) It is like no other rock in our yard. (3) It is brownish with some black and white. (4) It was near my favorite tree. And (5) The sun was shining on it. Ask your child what he or she would like you to write about his or her rock. Anything you and your child say will be appropriate!

If you have time, make up some games to play with your rocks. Each of you may then decide on a special place to save your rock.

✦ **Poetry Partners:** "Desert Tortoise," "maggie and milly and molly and may," "Growing Up," "Rules," and "I'm Glad the Sky Is Painted Blue" in *The Random House Book of Poetry for Children*; "My Rules" and "Stone Telling" in *Where the Sidewalk Ends*.

✦ **Related Books:** Also by Byrd Baylor: *The Desert is Theirs; Hawk, I'm Your Brother; I'm in Charge of Celebrations; If You Are a Hunter of Fossils; Moon Song;* and *Amigo*.

Book Share 29

*There is more treasure in books than in all
the pirate's loot on Treasure Island.*
—Walt Disney

Title: *26 Letters and 99 Cents*

Author: Tana Hoban

Publisher: Greenwillow

Summary: This book contains no words. If you start reading from one direction, you see photos of the letters of the alphabet and corresponding pictures. If you turn the book over and read from the other direction, you see photos of money, starting with a penny and going to 99 cents, with corresponding numbers. For the purposes of this reading of the book, only the alphabet selection will be used. However, don't neglect the counting/ money section. Children will enjoy it. This is a clever book, and parents and children get their money's worth as they explore the alphabet and how to count.

Key: Alphabet

◆ **Setting and Materials Needed:** The book sharing can take place in any comfortable setting. You will need a camera containing a roll of film with at least 26 exposures. You will also need 27 sheets of unlined paper and some glue or rubber cement. Finally, you will need a pad of lined paper.

◆ **Before Reading Activity:** Sing the alphabet song together to get warmed up for a close examination of the letters. Talk about what letters begin your name and your child's name. Say, "We are going to look at a book with the letters of the alphabet and some pictures of things that start with each letter."

◆ **During Reading Activity:** As you look at each page, say the letter and the name of the object in the corresponding picture. When you get to each of the letters in your child's first name, write the name of the picture down on your pad of paper and write your child's name below it. Underline the initial letter of the word representing the picture and underline that same letter in your child's name. Ask your child if they are the same letter, and tell him or her what the name of the letter is. If you know your child is aware of the letter name, have him or her tell you what it is.

✦ **After Reading Activity:**   Say to your child, "Let's make our own alphabet picture book." Put a large letter of the alphabet at the top of each of your blank sheets of paper. Say, "Let's take pictures of things that start with each of these letters. When we take a bunch of pictures, we'll have them developed and then we'll glue them on the paper and make our own picture alphabet book." Find objects in the house, outdoors, at a grandparent's house, and so on that represent the letters of the alphabet and take pictures of them. Be sure to take a picture of your son or daughter and have him or her take a picture of you. These pictures can be included in your book under the appropriate letter of the alphabet. This may take several days. When all the pictures have been taken and developed, look over *26 Letters and 99 Cents* again, and then glue your photos on the appropriate pages of your alphabet sheets. Have a title page saying something like "An Alphabet Picture Book by (your child's name)." Make sure the book is shared with lots of important and appreciative people.

✦ **Poetry Partners:**   "Alphabet Stew" in *The Random House Book of Poetry for Children*. The rest of the suggested poems are of things you might want to take pictures of: "Our House," "Our Washing Machine," "I've Got a Dog," "Cats," "My Little Sister," "Banananananananana" also in *The Random House Book of Poetry for Children*.

✦ **Related Books:**   *A Is for Angry* by Sandra Boynton; *Dr. Seuss's ABC* by Dr. Seuss; *A: My Name Is Alice* by Jane Bayer; other books by Tara Hoban are *1, 2, 3; Black on White;* and *White on Black.*

Book Share 30

I cannot live without books.
—Thomas Jefferson

Title: *Brown Bear, Brown Bear, What Do You See?*

Author: Bill Martin, Jr.

Illustrator: Eric Carle

Publisher: Henry Holt

Summary: This book has to be considered a classic in the predictable and pattern category. It is a story children love to have read to them and then love to pick up and "read" themselves. It begins, as well it should, "Brown Bear, Brown Bear, what do you see?" The brown bear sees a red bird who sees a yellow duck, with this pattern continuing through the body of the book.

Key: Predictable and Pattern

✦ **Setting and Materials Needed:** The book sharing should take place at any favorite reading location. You will need plain paper, something to write with, crayons, and three or four stuffed animals of, if possible, different colors.

✦ **Before Reading Activity:** Show your child the cover of the book. Ask your son or daughter what is on the cover. After he or she answers, read the title and ask, "What do you think the bear sees?" Be positive to any response. Then say, "Let's read the story to find out what the bear sees."

✦ **During Reading Activity:** As you read the first few pages, say to your child, "Look, each of the animals is a different color." Then point to the color of the animal as you read the corresponding color word of each animal.

✦ **After Reading Activity:** When you have finished reading the story, talk about all the things that were seen. Then say, "Listen to what I see. I see (your child's name) looking at me." Then say, "(Your child's name twice), what do you see?" Hopefully, your child will say, "I see my (mother or father) looking at me." If he or she is unwilling to respond say, "You are looking at me. Can you say, '(mom or dad) is looking at me?'" Then, write at the bottom on a plain piece of paper, *What (your child's name) sees*. Then, write on the bottom of the next sheet of paper, *(your child's name twice), what do you see?* Show your child one of the stuffed animals and ask what he or she sees. For example, your child might say, "I see a little mouse looking at me." Ask what color the mouse is and then write at the bottom of the next page, *I see a brown mouse looking at me*. Do this for three or four stuffed animals and then draw the pictures as best you can. Have your child color each picture appropriately. Staple the story together with the title sheet first and share it with all appropriate audiences (grandparents, aunts, uncles, brothers and sisters, and so forth).

✦ **Poetry Partners:** "Dogs and Cats and Bears and Bats," "Grandpa Bear's Lullaby," "The Blackbird," "Ducks' Ditty," "The Frog," "The Cats of Kilkenny," and "Sunning" in *The Random House Book of Poetry for Children*.

✦ **Related Books:** *Polar Bear, Polar Bear, What Do You Hear?; Here Are My Hands*, both by Bill Martin Jr. (He has many others.); *Big, Bad Bruce* by Bill Peet; *Friends* by Helen Oxenbury; and *Paddington Takes a Bath* and *Paddington at the Seashore* by Michael Bond.

Book Share 31

Many a book is like a key to unknown chambers within the castle of one's own self.
— Franz Kafka

Title: *Over in the Meadow*

Author: Ezra Jack Keats (based on original version by Olive A. Wadsworth)

Publisher: Scholastic

Summary: This is a story told in rhyme about animal mothers and their children. It begins in a meadow with a mother turtle and her "little turtle one." Each day introduces a new parent who has one more child than the preceding parent. This continues until we meet the mother firefly and her "little flies ten." She asks them to shine and shine they do. *Over in the Meadow* has a warm, summer-like feel.

Key: Predictable and Pattern

◆ **Setting and Materials Needed:** The book sharing should take place at any favorite reading location. It would be perfect, however, if it could be read in a park on an early summer's day. No special materials are needed but do not hesitate to take a picnic lunch.

◆ **Before Reading Activity:** As you sit in the sun (if, indeed, you have found a park on a sunny day), read the title and then explain what a meadow is. Tell your child it is like a big park, but it is usually located where there are not many people. Look at the cover, and ask if it looks like winter or summer. Then say, "Look at that animal. I wonder what it is? And are those its babies? Let's read and find out."

◆ **During Reading Activity:** After you read about the mother turtle and mother fish say, "The mother turtle had one baby and the mother fish had two babies. I wonder if the next mother will have three babies?" Read the next page about the mother bird and ask your child if the mother bird did have three babies. Then ask how many babies your child thinks the next animal will have. Read to find out but don't do any more guessing unless your child volunteers. Just enjoy the story.

✦ **After Reading Activity:**   Read the story again but, when you read about each animal, stop and you and your child count the number of babies on each page. Then talk about how many children are in your family. Discuss which page you would belong on. (If two children are in your family, you would be on the mother fish page because she has two babies). Talk about other families, human and animals, and how many children are involved.

✦ **Poetry Partners:**   "Little Bo-Peep," "The Clever Hen," "Two Birds," "Five Toes," "One, Two, Three," "The Robins," and "Baa, Baa Black Sheep" in *The Real Mother Goose*.

✦ **Related Books:**   *Animal Alphabet* by Doris Ehrlich; *Frog Went A-Courtin'* by Feodor Rojankovsky; *Have You Seen My Duckling?* by Nancy Tafuri; *Millions of Cats* by Wanda Gag; and *The Snowy Day* and *Jennie's Hat* by Ezra Jack Keats.

Book Share 32

*There are perhaps no days of our childhood we lived so
fully as those we believe we left without having lived
them, those we spent with a favorite book.*
—Marcel Proust

Title: *Albert's Alphabet*

Author: Leslie Tryon

Publisher: Aladdin

Summary: This clever alphabet book begins with Albert the goose, a
school carpenter, receiving a note from the principal of Pleasant Valley
School requesting that he build an alphabet on the walking path of the
school playground. In this mostly wordless book, Albert begins building the
letters using scraps of wood from his shop. When he runs out of wood, he
uses some very handy and unusual materials to construct the remaining
letters.

Key: Alphabet

✦ **Setting and Materials Needed:** Before you read this book with your child,
collect a variety of materials that you can use to construct letters of the alphabet. You might gather pebbles, toothpicks, sugar cubes, and string, for example. If you are handy with a hammer, nails, and wood scraps, they would provide a wonderful follow-up to the book. Place these objects in a bag on your
kitchen table for use after reading.

Find any comfortable place for reading, other than the kitchen.

✦ **Before Reading Activity:** Tell you child that you are going to read *Albert's
Alphabet*, the story of a goose that builds the letters of the alphabet for a
school. Ask your child to recite the letters of the alphabet with you. Praise his
or her attempts, and then begin sharing the book.

✦ **During Reading Activity:** This book has few words, so you will want to
talk through the pages with your child. Read the principal's letter. Then, on
pages 2 and 3, point to Albert's shop. Comment that he has some materials

that he might use to build the letters. What materials does he have? Notice the clock, and inform your child that Albert has only until 3 o'clock to construct all the letters. Point to the path where Albert will place the letters. Over the next several pages, enjoy Albert's skill in building the letters. Once he has finished the letters "M" and "N," talk about what he might use now that he has run out of wood. Again, pay attention to the clever manner in which Albert creates the letters. At the end of the book, point to the letters along the path and say them with your child.

✦ **After Reading Activity:** This book is a great springboard for building your own letters with your child. Take your child to the kitchen where you have assembled various materials in a bag. Ask him or her if you can build some letters together, and let him or her open to bag to see what you have placed inside. Build letters with your child, using the various materials and others, if your child has additional ideas. Your child may wish to start with "A" and work his or her way through the alphabet, as Albert did. Or, your child may wish to start with letters of particular importance or interest. For example, your child may want to build the letters that make up his or her name. Whatever you choose to do, have fun!

✦ **Poetry Partners:** "The Carpenter Rages," "Michael Built a Bicycle," and "Bulgy Bunne" in *The New Kid on the Block*; "Homemade Boat" in *Where the Sidewalk Ends*; "The Riveter" and "Concrete Mixers" in *The Random House Book of Poetry for Children*; and "London Bridge" in *The Real Mother Goose*.

✦ **Related Books:** Other books by Leslie Tryon include *Albert's Play*, *Albert's Field Trip*, and *Albert's Ball Game*. Books related to construction that your child might enjoy are *The Busy Building Book* by Sue Tarsky; *Building a House with Mr. Bumble* by John Wallace; and *Building a House* by Byron Barton.

Book Share 33

When I got [my] library card, that was when
my life began.
    —Rita Mae Brown

Title: *Sam and the Firefly*

Author: P. D. Eastman

Publisher: Random House

Summary: Sam, an owl, befriends a firefly named Gus and teaches him how to use his light to write words in the sky. They have fun until Gus decides to use his new trick to cause traffic problems by writing, "Go fast," "Go slow," "Go right," and "Go left" above a busy intersection. Sam tries to stop Gus, but Gus continues to be naughty, advertising free movies and cold (rather than hot) dogs. The angry Hot Dog Man captures Gus, puts him in a jar, and carries him off in his truck. When the truck stalls on a railroad track, Gus saves the day in a predictable way.

Key: Personal Value: Reading

◆ **Setting and Materials Needed:** You will need two flashlights for the before reading activity. This activity should be done in a dark room. Bedtime would be perfect. The after reading activity should be done the next day at a kitchen table or other convenient drawing place. You will need a yellow crayon, a black crayon, and a coin.

◆ **Before Reading Activity:** Sit in a dark room, or lie next to your child in bed. With the room lights off, turn on your flashlights. Play chase with your lights around the ceiling. Draw squiggly designs. Then tell your child that you are going to write some letters on the ceiling. Draw an "O." Ask your child if he or she could tell what the letter was. Draw an "L." If your child does not know the letters that you draw, tell him or her what they are. Have your child try drawing letters on the ceiling. Help him or her by holding his or her hand, if you need to. Write your names.

✦ **During Reading Activity:**   Tell your child that you are going to read a book about a firefly that writes words in the sky. Turn on the lights in the room and read the book. Our children loved this book, partly because fireflies are such fascinating creatures and partly because Gus is so naughty, but mostly because they enjoyed looking at the words Sam and Gus wrote in the sky. This "sky-writing" is a very attractive feature of the book. We found our children turning to those pages time and time again and reading the words to us. The book motivated our children to want to read and increased their awareness of and interest in print.

✦ **After Reading Activity:**   A fun after reading activity is to have your child color a piece of paper with a yellow crayon. It is important that you press hard with the crayon. Then after coloring with the yellow crayon, color over the yellow with a black crayon. Then use a coin to write letters in the "night sky." Scratch off the black crayon, revealing the yellow underneath. Spell your child's name in the sky. Write other important words in the sky.

✦ **Poetry Partners:**   "I wish I Could Meet the Man That Knows," "Poor Old Lady," "The Butterfly's Ball," "The Tickle Rhyme," "Clickbeetle," and "Hey, Bug!" from *The Random House Book of Poetry;* and "Magical Eraser" from *Where the Sidewalk Ends.*

✦ **Related Books:**   *Fireflies for Nathan* by Shulamith L. Oppenheim; *Fireflies in the Night* by Judy Hawes; *Fireflies!* by Julie Brinckloe; *Ten Flashing Fireflies* by Philemon Sturges; and *The Very Lonely Firefly* by Eric Carle. Another book by the author is *Are You My Mother?*

Book Share 34

A book is the best of friends,
the same today and forever.
　　—Martin Tupper

Title: *May I Bring a Friend?*

Author: Beatrice Schenk De Regniers

Illustrator: Beni Montresor

Publisher: Macmillan (Aladdin Books)

Summary: In this rhythmical, rhyming book, a child is invited each day of the week to visit the King and Queen. Each time he asks if he may bring a friend. The King and Queen say, "yes" and are surprised at some of their guests—a giraffe one day, a hippopotamus the next, and several monkeys later in the week! The King and Queen respond with good humor, and the story ends when they go to visit the boy and his friends at the zoo.

Key: Phonemic Awareness

◆ **Setting and Materials Needed:** Any comfortable setting will do.

◆ **Before Reading Activity:** Talk about those times when your child has been invited to go somewhere (a friend's house, a birthday party, to dinner). Tell him or her that you are about to read a story about a child who is invited to the home of the King and Queen. The child in the story asks if he may bring a friend. Who would your child invite to go with him or her if he or she were invited someplace special? After you've talked about this for a few minutes, look at the picture on the cover of the book. What does your child think is going on?

◆ **During Reading Activity:** After you have gotten to the point in the story where the boy has taken a giraffe and a hippopotamus, stop and ask what other animals your child thinks the boy might take to visit the King and Queen. On the last page, point to the words on the flags and read them to your child.

✦ **After Reading Activity:** Read the book a second time and pause before the rhyming words. Ask your child to predict what word fits at that point in the story. For instance, on the first page read, "The King and Queen invited me to come to their house on Sunday for _____." Do this throughout the book only if your child finds it interesting.

✦ **Poetry Partners:** Two poems about days of the week are "Sneezing" and "A Week of Birthdays" in *The Real Mother Goose*. Other related poems are "The Opposite of Two," "I Went to the Animal Fair," "Habits of the Hippopotamus," "The Lion," and "The Yak" in *The Random House Book of Poetry for Children*.

✦ **Related Books:** *If I Ran the Zoo* by Dr. Seuss; *Color Zoo* by Lois Ehlert; *Best Friends for Frances* by Russell Hoban; *Arthur's Birthday* by Marc Brown; *Frog and Toad Are Friends* by Arnold Lobel; *Who Will Be My Friends?* by Syd Hoff.

Book Share 35

*There are rainy afternoons in the country in autumn,
and stormy days in winter, when one's work outdoors is
finished and after wet clothes have been changed for dry,
the rocking-chair in front of the open woodfire simply
demands an accompanying book.*
—Theodore Roosevelt

Title: *Rain Talk*

Author: Mary Serfozo

Illustrator: Keiko Narahashi

Publisher: Scholastic

Summary: The author describes the various sounds of the rain as it falls on a dirt road, the tin roof of a garden shed, a pond, a highway, and other surfaces. A little girl listens to the sounds of the rain during the day and into the evening when she settles into bed. She awakens to a rainbow the next morning.

Key: Personal Value: Rainy days

✦ **Setting and Materials Needed:** This is an excellent book to read on a rainy day. The after reading activity takes place best in a bathtub. You will need water, pots, pans, paper, a piece of wood, and any other items you have handy and don't mind getting wet.

✦ **Before Reading Activity:** Walk around your home and listen to the sounds of the rain. How does it sound against the roof? How does it sound against the windows in your child's room? Stand on your porch or doorstep. How does the rain sound on the leaves of a plant, in the street, on puddles? Come back indoors and read *Rain Talk*.

✦ **During Reading Activity:** Enjoy the book with your child.

✦ **After Reading Activity:**   Do your after reading activity at bathtime. After your child steps into a full bathtub, turn the water on to dribble. Show your child the various items you have gathered and let him or her experiment with making the sounds of raindrops. What do the drops sound like falling into an empty pot or pan? What about a full one? What does the water sound like dripping on paper? How about a piece of wood? Children enjoy playing in water—let your child experiment. Read the book again while your child is in the tub. Try imitating the sounds in the book.

✦ **Poetry Partners:**   "Rain" and "Lazy Jane" from *Where the Sidewalk Ends;* "Mud," "The Muddy Puddle," "Rain Clouds," "To Walk in Warm Rain," and "April Rain Song" from *The Random House Book of Poetry for Children.*

✦ **Related Books:**   *Bringing the Rain to Kapiti Plain: A Nandi Tale* by Verna Aardema; *A Drop of Rain* by Wong Yee; *Down Comes the Rain* by Franklyn Branley; *The Snowy Day* by Ezra Jack Keats; *It Rained on the Desert Today* by Ken and Debby Buchanan; *Listen to the Rain* by Bill Martin, Jr. and John Archambault.

Book Share 36

Through engagement with others, literature lets us
imagine what it would be like to be different.
　　—Denis Donoghue

Title: *Someone Special, Just Like You*

Authors: Tricia Brown

Photographer: Fran Ortiz

Publisher: Henry Holt

Summary: This book of photographs and text depicts children who may not walk, talk, hear, or see the way other children do. The photos were taken at four preschools. The text presents these children in a sensitive manner. This is an important book as it helps children understand that physical differences are not as important as the things we all have in common, the things that make us all special.

Key: Personal Value: Children with disabilities

✦ **Setting and Materials Needed:** The book sharing should take place at the kitchen or dining room table. No materials are needed.

✦ **Before Reading Activity:** Talk with your child about some of the things you find really special about him or her. You might want to mention that you like his or her special hug, smile, or kiss because each of these is discussed at the end of the book. Show your child the cover of *Someone Special, Just Like You* and read the title. Say, "The book says these are special children . . . just like you. Let's read the book to find out why they are special."

✦ **During Reading Activity:** To fully appreciate the message, slowly read the text straight through. This allows your child to understand more easily the important message. Reading it slowly gives your child the opportunity to look at the photographs and notice that the children pictured are special. Read the story again and take time to look at the pictures together. If your child wants to know why individuals pictured cannot walk, or see, or hear, tell them you are not sure. Be open to discussing possible causes. Then say, "I bet he or she likes (mention your child's favorite ice cream) just like you do." Focus on what the children pictured and your child have in common.

✦ **After Reading Activity:** Say, "What a special book about special kids. I especially liked reading it with you." Then give your child a hug, kiss, or smile, or, better yet, give all three!

✦ **Poetry Partners:** "The Wrong Start," "I Wish I Could Meet the Man That Knows," "Up in the Pine," "Two People," "Everybody Says," "The Reason I Like Chocolate," and "Hug O'War" in *The Random House Book of Poetry for Children.*

✦ **Related Books:** There is an extensive list of suggested books to read to your child at the conclusion of *Someone Special, Just like You.* The books presented are in the following categories: deaf, hearing-impaired, and physical, mental, and visual disabilities.

Book Share 37

To read a book properly is to wake up and live, to acquire a renewed interest in one's neighbors, more especially those who are alien to us in every way.
    —Henry Miller

Title: *Amazon Alphabet*

Author: Tanis Jordan

Illustrator: Martin Jordan

Publisher: Kingfisher

Summary: A rain forest animal is depicted for each letter of the alphabet. The pronunication of each animal's name is provided at the bottom of the page on which it is found, and fascinating information about the animals is found at the end of the book.

Key: Alphabet

◆ **Setting and Materials Needed:** Alphabet refrigerator magnets or letter cards are needed for the after reading activity. If you have neither of these, you can make a set of letter cards by writing the letters of the alphabet on index cards or pieces of paper.

◆ **Before Reading Activity:** Before reading this alphabet book, sit behind your child and draw a letter of the alphabet on his or her back using your finger. Ask your child to guess what letter you are drawing. Do this several times. You may find your child squealing with delight. Then, let your child draw letters on your back while you guess.

   Tell your child that you are going to read an alphabet book, one that shares a jungle animal for each letter. Explain that the Amazon jungle is in South America, showing your child on a map or globe where this region is. The Amazon is home to many interesting animals, some of which will be shared in this book.

✦ **During Reading Activity:**   Read this book, pointing to each word as you read it. Emphasize the letter sound at the beginning of the animal name ("A is for *Agouti* . . . " "F is for *Frog* . . . ") as you point to the letter at the beginning of the word. Read as much information from the back of the book as interests your child. Remember that you are building background knowledge when you share the information about each of these interesting animals, as well as developing a positive attitude about exploring our world, so do not omit this portion of the book unless your child is obviously unwilling to listen.

✦ **After Reading Activity:**   After reading the book, have some fun with the alphabet. Go to your refrigerator and play with the letter magnets. (Or, use letter cards, spreading them out on the floor or a table.) Ask your child to find letters that you call out. Use words from the *Amazon Alphabet* book—"F is for frog. Can you find an F?" After you have called the letters for awhile, have your child name letters for you to find. Then, if your child is interested, put some letters together to spell words. Use familiar words, such as your child's name, "mom," "dad," and "cat," that your child may be able to recognize.

✦ **Poetry Partners:**   "The Bat," "The Sloth," "Four Little Foxes," "Green Stems," "The Frog," "The Tree Frog," and "The Hummingbird" all from *The Random House Book of Poetry for Children.*

✦ **Related Books:**   *A Walk in the Rain Forest, A Fly in the Sky,* and *A Swim through the Sea* all by Kristin Joy Pratt; *A Is for Africa* by Ifeoma Onyefulu; *Alaska ABC Book* by Charlene Kreeger and Shannon Cartwright; *C Is for China* by Sungwan So.

Book Share 38

In reading, appetite is half the feast.
—*Celebrating the National Reading Initiative*

Title: *The Hungry Thing*

Authors: Jan Slepian and Ann Seidler

Illustrator: Richard E. Martin

Publisher: Scholastic

Summary: If there is such a thing as a classic book in the phonemic awareness area, *The Hungry Thing* is it. The Hungry Thing comes to a town with a sign around his neck saying "Feed Me." When the townspeople ask what he would like to eat, he says, "shmancakes." The townspeople are baffled until a little boy indicates that "shmancakes" sounds like pancakes. This continues with tickles, feetloaf, and so on. Children have a great time guessing the foods the Hungry Thing wants.

Key: Phonemic Awareness

◆ **Setting and Materials Needed:** The book sharing should take place at the kitchen or dining room table. You will need lined paper and a pencil with a good eraser.

◆ **Before Reading Activity:** This activity would take place best before the noon or evening meal. Tell your child you are making some food with silly sounding names. Say, "First, I'm going to give you something to drink. It's called 'gilk.'" Then give him or her a glass of milk. Next say, "Now I want to give you something to eat. It's called 'baghetti.'" Then give your child some spaghetti. Say, "I'm putting a different sound at the beginning of foods you like. I think it's fun. Let's do it some more." Do the same thing with other appropriate foods. Finally, state, "Let's read a book about a hungry thing (show the cover) and see what he likes to eat."

✦ **During Reading Activity:**   As you read the story, don't worry about your child guessing on the first two foods the Hungry Thing wants. But when you get to "feetloaf," ask your child to guess what the Hungry Thing wants as you finish the sentence. "Feetloaf . . . sounds like Beetloaf . . . sounds like _____." (Have your child guess here). If he or she doesn't want to make a guess you might think aloud what you think it is. "Let's see, feetloaf, what do people eat that sounds like feetloaf? Could it be deetloaf? No, that doesn't sound right. Could it be zeetloaf? No! I know, I think it is meatloaf!" In this way you provide a model for the way your son or daughter might think about the food the Hungry Thing really wants.

✦ **After Reading Activity:**   Talk about what a fun book *The Hungry Thing* is. Then ask your child if he or she wants to prepare a menu the Hungry Thing might put together. Start with what you would have for a drink. Write the word down. Then erase the first letter and talk with your son or daughter about a sound that might be put there. For example, write down orange juice. Erase the "j" from juice and say, "What can we put in front of uice? Should we have buice or huice or muice?" Which would the Hungry Thing like best?" Continue with other foods including dessert. Share the menu with others in the family and see if they can guess the foods.

You also may wish to put some food in a bag and encourage your child to guess what you have. Give your child a rhyming clue. "It's a ganana." Let your child guess, then pull the food from the bag. Let your child do the same for you. Alternatively, you may wish to stand together in front of an open refrigerator or pantry, like two Hungry Things, and give food items new names, modeling the pattern in the book.

Poetry Partners: "Lazy Jane," "Skinny," "Fish?" "Peanut-Butter Sandwich," "With His Mouth Full of Food," "Pancake?" and "Hungry Mungry" in *Where the Sidewalk Ends.*

✦ **Related Books:**   *Benny Bakes a Cake* by Eve Rice; *The Hungry Little Boy* by Joan W. Blos; *Alphabite!: A Funny Feast from A to Z* by Charles Reasoner; *Bread and Jam for Frances* by Russell Hoban; *Lunch* by Denise Fleming; and *Who Ate It?* by Taro Gomi.

Book Share 39

People can lose their lives in libraries.
They ought to be warned.
—Saul Bellow

Title: *Five Little Monkeys Sitting in a Tree*

Author: Eileen Christelow

Publisher: Clarion

Summary: Five little monkeys and their mama go to the river for a picnic. The little monkeys climb a tree and tease Mr. Crocodile in the river below. He snaps at the monkeys, and soon only four little monkeys are sitting in the tree teasing Mr. Crocodile. Then three, two, one, and finally no little monkeys are left to tease Mr. Crocodile. Their mama panics, but then sees that the five little monkeys are hiding safely among the branches. They come down and eat their supper and never tease Mr. Crocodile again.

Key: Predictable and Pattern

✦ **Setting and Materials Needed:** Any location is fine for reading this fun book. You will need six toy animals—preferably five monkeys and a crocodile!—but any six animals will do.

✦ **Before Reading Activity:** Many young children know the rhyme about the five little monkeys jumping on the bed. It goes like this:

> *Five little monkeys jumping on a bed*
> *One fell off and hurt his head*
> *Mama called the doctor, and the doctor said,*
> *"No more monkeys jumping on the bed!"*

> *Four little monkeys jumping on the bed*
> *One fell off and hurt his head*
> *Mama called the doctor, and the doctor said,*
> *"No more monkeys jumping on the bed!"*

This chant repeats, counting down to three, two, and one little monkey jumping on the bed.

Say this rhyme with your child. Then tell your child that you are going to read a story about five little monkeys who get in trouble at a picnic.

✦ **During Reading Activity:** This rhythmic book is especially enjoyable when read as a chant. Read it several times with your child. The first time, just enjoy the story. The second time, encourage your child to look at the pictures and count the monkeys remaining on the branch after each snap from Mr. Crocodile. Also, if your child hasn't noticed already, assist him or her in finding the illustrator's clues that the little monkeys are, indeed, safe. Ask your child, "Did Mr. Crocodile really eat that little monkey?" If your child is not sure, ask him or her to look carefully at the picture and, if necessary, help your child find evidence of the hidden monkey. After you have helped your child once, he or she will have fun finding the hidden monkeys on the remaining pages of the book. Finally, read the book slowly a third time, pausing in predictable places so your child can join in the story.

✦ **After Reading Activity:** Act out the story with your child's toys as you recite the rhyme together. You may need to change the rhyme to "Five little animals." And, if you do not have a toy crocodile, change the rhyme to match whatever animal you choose to replace the crocodile.

✦ **Poetry Partners:** "Nine Mice" from *The New Kid on the Block;* "One, Two, Three," "Two Birds," and "Five Toes" in *The Real Mother Goose;* "The Acrobats" and "The Crocodile's Toothache" in *Where the Sidewalk Ends;* "The Crocodile" in *The Random House of Poetry for Children.*

✦ **Related Books:** *Five Little Monkeys Jumping on the Bed* and *Don't Wake Up Mama* by Eileen Christelow; *Caps for Sale* by Esphyr Slobodkina; *How Many, How Many, How Many* by Rick Walton; *1,2,3 to the Zoo* by Eric Carle; and *The Doorbell Rang* by Pat Hutchins.

Book Share 40

The smallest bookstore still contains more ideas of worth than have been presented in the entire history of television . . .
—Andrew Ross

Title: *Ten Cats Have Hats*

Author: Jean Marzollo

Illustrator: David McPhail

Publisher: Scholastic

Summary: In this counting book, a child identifies the possessions of one bear, two ducks, three trees, and so on through the number ten. Both rhyme and repetition are key features in the story. Each owner rhymes with its possession: The bear has a chair, the ducks have trucks, and the trees have bees. At the conclusion of each page, the child proudly announces, "but I have a hat."

Key: Phonemic Awareness

✦ **Setting and Materials Needed:** You will need several small, familiar objects. These might include a nickel, a toy plane, a small stuffed animal, a rock, a pen, and a spoon. Almost any small object will do, and a quick search inside and outside your home will provide more than enough objects. Put these objects in a hat for sharing after reading. You will need two additional hats to be worn throughout the experience.

✦ **Before Reading Activity:** Tell your child the name of the book and then suggest that you each wear a hat while reading the story about a child who has many different hats. Discuss the features (such as color and shape) of your hats.

✦ **During Reading Activity:** Read the story through once in its entirety. Then read it again more slowly. This time stop to count the objects on each page. Notice that on every page the child is wearing a different hat. You might pause just before the rhyming word. This will encourage your child to predict it before you read it. You might also pause each time during the line "But I have a (pause) hat." Your child is likely to find this an easy word to contribute to the reading.

✦ **After Reading Activity:**   Surprise your child with the hat that contains the objects you collected earlier. Tell your child that together you are going to create your own story similar to the one you just read. Let your child look into the hat and select any object. He or she should hold the object and, with your help, say a rhyme following the general pattern in the book. For instance, your child might look into the hat and grab the nickel. With your support, he or she might say, "One nickel has a pickle!" (Nonsense words such as "zickle," "wickle," and "bickle" are acceptable, too!) Then look at each other and say, "But we have hats!" Repeat this pattern for as many of the objects in the hat as your child wishes. Each time be sure to say, "But we have hats!"

If you have only one of each item in the hat, this obviously will not be a counting activity. Each time your child selects something from the hat, he or she will use the number one. If you would like to incorporate the counting aspect of the book in this activity, you will need to gather more than one of some of the objects. You might find two dimes, three rocks, four pencils, and so on. Let your child search through the hat to find the objects for each number.

If you are both enjoying the activity, empty the hat of your selections, and encourage your child to fill the hat with objects of his or her own choosing.

✦ **Poetry Partners:**   "Tight Hat" and "Hat" in *Where the Sidewalk Ends*; "A Counting-Out Rhyme," "One, Two, Buckle My Shoe," "One, He Loves," "Two Birds," and "One, Two, Three" in *The Real Mother Goose*.

✦ **Related Books:**   Books about hats include *Jennie's Hat* by Ezra Jack Keats; *Whose Hat Is That?* by Ron Roy; *The Hat* by Jan Brett; and *The Cat in the Hat* by Dr. Seuss. Counting books include *Anno's Counting Book* by Mitsumasa Anno and *Fish Eyes: A Book You Can Count On* by Lois Ehlert.

Book Share 41

*A book is a part of life . . . just as much as
a tree or a horse or a star.*
—Henry Miller

Title: *The Monster Book of ABC Sounds*

Author: Alan Snow

Publisher: Penguin

Summary: Rats look for monster friends in a fun game of hide-and-seek. As the monsters are discovered in their varied and interesting hiding places, sounds of the alphabet are heard: "Aaaah!" scream the rats when they find the first monster in a cupboard; "Mmmm" says the monster who is caught eating honey in the pantry. Children will enjoy the illustrations in this rhyming alphabet book.

Key: Alphabet

◆ **Setting and Materials Needed:** You will need letter cards. You can make these by writing a capital letter on one side of an index card and the small letter on the back side: "A" on one side, "a" on the other side; "B" on one side of another card, "b" on the other side, and so forth. If you do not have index cards handy, you may simply cut paper to that approximate size. Be sure not to cut the pieces of paper too small, as they will be used in a game of hide-and-seek and you want your child to be able to find them.

◆ **Before Reading Activity:** Play a game of traditional hide-and-seek with your child. After you have played for awhile, settle into a comfortable chair together and tell your child that you are going to read an alphabet book about monsters and rats that play hide-and-seek together.

◆ **During Reading Activity:** There is a lot to this book. The rhythm of the author's language and the rhymes make the story enjoyable and the reading poetic. The illustrations contribute much to the story, and children should have the opportunity to explore them. They will want to talk about the monsters' hiding places and look at the details on each page. Additionally, the letters and letter sounds are important features of the book. Because of this complexity, the book should be read several times. First, read the book to enjoy the story. Begin by reading the first two pages. Then point to and say the rat's response to finding the first monster ("Aaaah!"). Then read the second two pages before pointing to the monster's and rats' responses ("Boo!" and "Cooee!"). Reading in this manner will allow your child to attend to the story and hear the rhyming pattern. If your child insists upon stopping and talking about each page, do not hesitate to do so. Be responsive to his or her interests.

On a second reading of the book, point out the letters of the alphabet in the corner and around the border of each page. You also may wish to point out that each exclamation from a rat or monster is the sound the letter makes (on the "s" page, a slithery monster says, "Ssssss") or begins with the sound the letter makes (on the "q" page, a monster says "quack").

Finally, if you look closely, you will find alphabetically appropriate items on each page. Finding them all is a challenge that you might undertake on a third look at the book.

✦ **After Reading Activity:**   After reading this book, play hide-and-seek with your child again. This time, hide alphabet cards around the house or yard while your child is closing his or her eyes and counting. You might want to hide all 26 cards or only a few, depending on your child's interest in this activity. Have your child hunt for the cards. When your child finds a card, he or she brings it to you and tells you the letter name, the sound the letter makes, or a word that begins with the sound the letter makes, whichever you feel your child is able to do successfully. If you choose to play with all the alphabet cards, let your child try putting them in order on the ground after they are found. When you're finished, let your child hide the cards for you!

✦ **Poetry Partners:**   "The Yipiyuk," "The Bloath," and "The Worst" from *Where the Sidewalk Ends;* "There Is a Thing" and "Its Fangs Were Red" from *The New Kid on the Block;* and "What's That?" and "Ms. Whatchamacallit Thingama-jig" from *The Random House Book of Poetry for Children.*

✦ **Related Books:**   Another alphabet book is *Alison's Zinnia* by Anita Lobel. Favorite monster books include *Little Monster Goes on Safari* and *There's a Nightmare in My Closet,* both by Mercer Mayer; *Where the Wild Things Are* by Maurice Sendak; *My Mama Says There Aren't Any Zombies, Ghosts, Vampires, Creatures, Demons, Monsters, Fiends, Goblins, or Things* by Judith Viorst; and *Clyde Monster* by Robert Crowe and Kay Chorao.

Book Share 42

The great gift is the passion for reading. It is cheap, it consoles, it distracts, it excites. It gives you knowledge of the world and experiences of a wide kind.
—Elizabeth Hardwick

Title: *The Fox Went Out on a Chilly Night*

Author: Peter Spier

Publisher: Picture Yearling

Summary: An old song, *The Fox Went Out on a Chilly Night,* tells the story of a fox who heads to town (town-o, town-o, town-o) to get some food for his family. He catches and carries off a goose and a duck (with their legs dangling down-o, down-o, down-o), but is spotted by old mother Giggle-Gaggle who alerts her husband to his presence. The fox races homeward before the others are on his tail-o, and he and his wife eat a fine dinner while their little ones chew on the bones-o, bones-o, bones-o.

Key: Phonemic Awareness

✦ **Setting and Materials Needed:** Any comfortable setting will do. An index card with the letter "o" printed on it is needed.

✦ **Before Reading Activity:** Tell your child that this is actually an old song about a fox that goes out to find some food for its family. Alert your child to the fact that the author does something amusing with sounds to make the story even more interesting.

✦ **During Reading Activity:** Enjoy the story. When you get to the first point where the /o/ is added to a word, smile and say, "See how the author adds a sound here to make this interesting?" Continue to note the use of /o/ at the end of words throughout this story.

✦ **After Reading Activity:**   Talk about the use of the /o/ sound and how it added pleasure and humor to the story/song. Think of other words you might add /o/ to for fun. Give your child the card with the letter "o." Tell her or him that this is the letter that was added to words to make the /o/ sound at the end. Find a page in the book that does this, and point to this letter. Then encourage your child to touch various objects around the room with the card. Each time he or she touches an object with the letter, you say the word for that object with the /o/ addition. For example, if your child touches a book with the "o" card, you say "book-o." If he or she touches a desk or a door, you say "desk-o," "door-o," respectively. You take a turn at touching objects with the "o" card and let your child say the new word. Do this as long as your child finds it fun. You may wish at some future reading to introduce other cards, such as "a" or "i" and make these sound additions to words (e.g., book-a, desk-a, door-a). Share some of the poems listed below that make use of sound addition.

✦ **Poetry Partners:**   "Antonio," "Mr. Bidery's Spidery Garden," "Sing Me a Song of Teapots and Trumpets," "The Bluffalo," "Moses," "Habits of the Hippopotamus," and "Four Seasons" in *The Random House Book of Poetry for Children*.

✦ **Related Books:**   *Fox in Socks* by Dr. Seuss; *Rosie's Walk* by Pat Hutchins; *Flossie and the Fox* by Patricia C. McKissack; *Doctor De Soto* by William Steig; *Grandfather Tang's Story* by Ann Tompert; and *The Tale of Jemima Puddle-Duck* by Beatrix Potter.

Book Share 43

*I have always imagined that Paradise
will be kind of a library.*
—Jorge Luis Borges

Title: *Clifford's Halloween*

Author: Norman Bridwell

Publisher: Four Winds

Summary: Clifford is a big red dog, not just any big red dog but a *really* big red dog. Emily Elizabeth, his owner, thinks he is the most special dog in the world—and she could be right. In *Clifford's Halloween*, Emily Elizabeth is trying to decide what she wants to be on Halloween. She also remembers past Halloweens and the problems Clifford, because of his size, caused. At the end of the story, she is trying to decide what Clifford should be on Halloween. She asks the reader, "What do you suggest?"

Key: Personal Value: Halloween

✦ **Setting and Materials Needed:** The book sharing should take place at any comfortable or favorite reading place. No materials are needed.

✦ **Before Reading Activity:** Look at the cover of *Clifford's Halloween*. Ask your child what time of the year it is. Once he or she guesses correctly, read the title and ask your child who he or she thinks Clifford is. Hopefully your child will think Clifford is the big red dog on the cover. Say, "Do you think it would be fun to have a dog like Clifford on Halloween?" Discuss this question, and then say, "Let's read the story to find out what a Halloween with Clifford might be like."

✦ **During Reading Activity:** Read the story straight through until Emily asks, "What do you think Clifford should be?" Spend time discussing some options. Don't hesitate to give your opinion. This can serve as a model for what your child might say. When you both have voiced some Halloween options, read the final few pages. Enjoy Emily's suggestions together.

✦ **After Reading Activity:**   After the book has been read, discuss some advantages and disadvantages to having Clifford along on Halloween. Look back through the book to gain some ideas. Then, if you have a pet in the house, discuss some good costumes for this pet on Halloween.

✦ **Poetry Partners:**   "Me and My Giant," "Colors," "The Loser," "Jimmy Jet and His TV Set," "Enter the Deserted House," "The Flying Festoon," and "If I Had a Brontosaurus" in *Where the Sidewalk Ends.*

✦ **Related Books:**   *Clifford, The Big Red Dog, Clifford's ABC,* and *The Witch Next Door,* all by Norman Bridwell; *What Is Halloween?* by Harriet Ziefert; *Big Pumpkin* by Erica Silverman; and *Boo! It's Halloween* by Wendy Watson.

Book Share 44

*Reading is a pleasure of the mind, which means that
it is a little like a sport; your eagerness and knowledge
and quickness count for something. The fun of reading
is not that something is told you, but that you stretch
your mind.*

    —Bennett Cerf

Title: *Owl Moon*

Author: Jane Yolen

Illustrator: John Schoenherr

Publisher: Philomel

Summary: This is a beautifully illustrated story of a child who goes owling with her father for the first time. "If you go owling, you have to be quiet," her father tells her, and so they walk through the cold woods without making a sound, except for the crunching of their feet in the snow and the who-who-whooing of the father calling out to owls. Finally, his calls are answered by a Great Horned Owl, and they catch the owl in their flashlight and stare into his eyes for "one minute, three minutes, maybe a hundred minutes" before he flies away.

Key: Personal Value: Nature

✦ **Setting and Materials Needed:** This is a good bedtime book. You will begin the sharing experience outdoors. Then go indoors, settle into your favorite reading spot, and cuddle under a blanket as you enjoy the story. If you ever go camping, take this book along.

✦ **Before Reading Activity:** Go outside and listen to the nighttime sounds. Try to identify the sounds, especially the sounds of animals. Depending on where you live, you might hear crickets, owls, frogs, or other animals. Tell your child that some animals sleep during the day and are awake at night, and that some people enjoy watching these night animals. Tell your child that this is the story of a child whose father takes her owling.

✦ **During Reading Activity:** This is a beautiful book. As you enjoy the author's language, also take the time to enjoy the illustrations, especially the details. Children love finding the train in the background on the first pages of the story, for example. As you read in a quiet place and a soft voice to match the mood of the story, encourage your child to try making the owl calls with you.

You may wish to point to the words when you read "Whoo-Whoo-Who-Who-Who-Whooooooo." Note how you say the word longer when the author writes it longer.

✦ **After Reading Activity:** Before bedtime on the next day, go outside and try calling for owls. Listen carefully—your calls might get answered! Go indoors and read the book again.

✦ **Poetry Partners:** "An Unassuming Owl" from *The New Kid on the Block*; "Owl," "The Owl and the Pussycat," "Wind-Wolves," "A Wolf . . . " and "Night Heron" from *The Random House Book of Poetry for Children*; "The Boy in the Barn" in *The Real Mother Goose*.

✦ **Related Books:** *Owl at Home* by Arnold Lobel; *Owl Babies* by Martin Waddell; *Owl (See How They Grow)* by Mary Ling; and *The Tale of Squirrel Nutkin* by Beatrix Potter. Also by Jane Yolen is *Sea Watch: A Book of Poetry*. John Schoenherr, who illustrated *Owl Moon*, has written and illustrated a book entitled *Bear*, which your child will enjoy.

Book Share 45

Books never annoy; they cost little, and they are always at hand, and ready for your call.
—William Cobbett

Title: *A You're Adorable*

Authors: Buddy Kaye, Fred Wise, and Sidney Lippman

Illustrator: Martha Alexander

Publisher: Candlewick

Summary: This popular song from the 1940s is illustrated with children, infants, and animals climbing on and through each letter of the alphabet. The music for the song is provided.

Key: Alphabet

✦ **Setting and Materials Needed:** Alphabet cards are needed for the after reading activity.

✦ **Before Reading Activity:** Sing the traditional alphabet song ("ABCDE FG . . . " to the tune of "Twinkle, Twinkle, Little Star") with your child. Then tell him or her that other songs have been written using the alphabet. This book shares one of those songs.

✦ **During Reading Activity:** Sing your way through the book, tracing each letter with your finger as you go. Repeat the entire book, this time holding your child's finger in your hand.

✦ **After Reading Activity:** After reading the book, sing the song with your child. Set out the letters of the alphabet in order and ask your child to pick up each letter as it is introduced in the song. Then try mixing up the letters and while you sing slowly, let your child hunt for the letter to hold up.

   You may wish to think of other words for the song. For example, "A, you're my apple pie; B, you're the best I know; C, you're a cuddly little dear."

◆ **Poetry Partners:** "I Love You," "Love," "Question," "Somebody," "Huckleberry, Gooseberry, Raspberry Pie," and "Some Things Don't Make Any Sense at All" in *The Random House Book of Poetry for Children*; "ABC" in *The Real Mother Goose*.

◆ **Related Books:** Other songs presented as books include *The Wheels on the Bus* by Paul O. Zelinsky; *Frog Went A-Courtin'* by Feodor Rojankovsky and John Langstaff; *Go Tell Aunt Rhody* by Aliki; *This Old Man* by Carol Jones; *I Know an Old Lady Who Swallowed a Fly* by Nadine Westcott; and *Down by the Bay* by Raffi.

Book Share 46

*I like books. I was born and bred among them, and
have the easy feeling, when I get into their presence,
that a stable-boy has among horses.*
—Oliver Wendell Holmes

Title: *Alexander and the Terrible, Horrible,
No Good, Very Bad Day*

Author: Judith Viorst

Illustrator: Ray Cruz

Publisher: Atheneum

Summary: The title, while lengthy, is a great description of the story. The main character, Alexander, is in school but this is still a story most preschoolers easily relate to. Alexander has a very bad day. He awakes with gum in his hair, and things go downhill from there. When things get particularly bad, he voices a predictable refrain, "I think I'll move to Australia." As he slips into bed in the evening, the bad day continues, and the story ends with Alexander saying, "My mom says some days are like that . . . even in Australia."

Key: Predictable and Pattern

✦ **Setting and Materials Needed:** The book sharing should take place at any favorite reading location. As a bedtime story *Alexander* is especially effective. No materials are needed.

✦ **Before Reading Activity:** Read your child the title of the book. Ask your son or daughter why he or she thinks Alexander might have had a terrible, horrible, no good, very bad day. You might want to suggest some things that could make a bad day if your child is unwilling to volunteer some ideas. For example, you might say, "I wonder if Alexander didn't get any breakfast? Maybe he broke a favorite toy? What could make a really bad day?" After your child has guessed and you have told him or her "What good guesses," say, "Let's read the story to find out why Alexander had a terrible, horrible, no good, very bad day."

✦ **During Reading Activity:** As you read the story, make a slight pause just before Australia each time Alexander says, "I think I'll move to (pause) Australia" and just before "day" in the phrase, "I could tell it was going to be a terrible, horrible, no good very bad (pause) day."

✦ **After Reading Activity:** When you have finished reading the story, talk about Alexander's really bad day. Go back and look at some of the pictures that show some of the things you talk about. Then say, "Let's talk about what would happen in a really good day. Let's call it (your child's name) and the fun, wonderful, really great, really special day." Then, just talk about what makes a special day and say, "Let's try, tomorrow, to do some of the special things we've talked about." The next day, try to do one or two of the special things you and your child discussed. Don't hesitate, on especially bad days for your child or the family, to bring out and read *Alexander*.

✦ **Poetry Partners:** "I've Got an Itch," "Never Mince Words with a Shark," "No, I Won't Turn Orange," "Sneaky Sue," "What Nerve You've Got, Minerva Mott," "Today Is Very Boring," and "I Found a Four-Leaf Clover" in *The New Kid on the Block*.

✦ **Related Books:** *Alexander, Who Used to Be Rich Last Sunday, I'll Fix Anthony,* and *Alphabet from Z to A (with Much Confusion on the Way)*, all by Judith Viorst (she has many others); *Pierre* and *Where The Wild Things Are* by Maurice Sendak; and *The Berenstain Bears and Too Much TV* by Stan and Jan Berenstain.

Book Share 47

*I have never known any distress that
an hour's reading did not relieve.*

—Montesquieu

Title: *Each Peach Pear Plum*

Author: Janet and Allan Ahlberg

Publisher: Viking

Summary: On each page of this rhyming book, the listener is asked to spy a nursery rhyme character in the accompanying picture: "Each Peach Pear Plum, I spy Tom Thumb." Tom Thumb can be found sitting in a peach tree. Careful examination of some pictures is necessary to find the hidden character. For instance, just the arm and hand of Cinderella, holding a feather duster, are visible. This makes the spy game more challenging and more delightful.

Key: Phonemic Awareness

✦ **Setting and Materials Needed:** Any comfortable setting will do.

✦ **Before Reading Activity:** Tell your child that this book brings together many familiar characters from a variety of stories and nursery rhymes. You and your child will meet Cinderella, the Three Bears, Jack and Jill, Little Bo Peep, and others in a single book. You may even wish to read a few of the nursery rhymes whose characters appear in this story before reading the book.

✦ **During Reading Activity:** Take time to look carefully at each picture as you read this book. Let your child spy the character referred to on each page.

✦ **After Reading Activity:** Play "I Spy" games with your child. Begin by looking around the room and providing clues, such as color and function. "I spy something brown, made out of wood, that we sit in" (a rocking chair). Let your child take turns giving you clues. Next, provide sound clues. "I spy something in the room that begins like this: /sh/" (shoe). "I spy something out the window that begins like this: /ss/" (swing). One of our daughters likes her parents to say the whole word by sounds: "I spy your /d/-/o/-/ll/" (doll). "I spy a /b-/ir/-/d/" (bird). Be playful and positive as you encourage your child to think about sounds.

✦ **Poetry Partners:** "Old Mother Hubbard," "Bye, Baby Bunting," "Little Bo-Peep," "Jack and Jill," and "Robin Hood and Little John" in *The Real Mother Goose;* "Eight Witches" and "One Day When We Went Walking" in *The Random House Book of Poetry for Children.*

✦ **Related Books:** *The Jolly Postman* and *The Jolly Christmas Postman* also by Janet and Allan Ahlberg; *The Stinky Cheese Man and Other Fairly Stupid Tales* by Jon Scieszka and Lane Smith; *Where's Waldo?* by Martin Handford; *I Spy: A Book of Picture Riddles* and *I Spy Fantasy: A Book of Picture Riddles,* both by Jean Marzollo and Walter Wick.

Book Share 48

I cannot sleep unless I am surrounded by books.
—Jorge Luis Borges

Title: *There's a Wocket in My Pocket*

Author: Dr. Seuss

Publisher: Random House

Summary: Many Dr. Seuss books are built around play with language. In this story, a child describes the kind of house he lives in—one where there is a "woset in the closet," "a zamp in the lamp," and a "nooth grush" on his toothbrush—and concludes that he hopes to never leave it.

Key: Phonemic Awareness

◆ **Setting and Materials Needed:** Several sheets of paper and crayons will be needed. The story should be read in a room where a table or flat surface is available.

◆ **Before Reading Activity:** Select a room in your house where you will be comfortable reading and drawing. Ask your child to name the objects in the room (e.g., rug, books, chair). See how many objects you can name together. Tell your child that the book you are going to read is about the objects in someone's house and the unusual creatures who live there!

◆ **During Reading Activity:** Read the story. After the pattern of rhyme has become clear, add a pause in your reading long enough to encourage your child to predict the rhyming word that identifies the location of the creature. You may wish to add a slight emphasis to the rhyme partner. For example, "The one I'm really scared of is that *Zug* (slight emphasis) under the (pause) rug" or "And that *Quimney* (slight emphasis) up the (pause) chimney." Use the pause to encourage predictions, but do not demand them. It is likely to be difficult for children to predict correctly on the first reading of the book.

✦ **After Reading Activity:**   After reading the story, talk about what unusual creatures could be found in your house. Support your child's attempts to make up words that rhyme with household objects ("There's a toor on the door.") Use the crayons to draw pictures of your made-up creatures together (the sillier, the better!), talking about them while drawing. Ask your child if he or she wishes you to write the name of each creature drawn. Drawings can be shared later with any appreciative audience.

You also may wish to go on a "creature hunt" throughout your house. Hold hands and tiptoe from room to room and point at various imaginary creatures, "Look, there's a ned on my bed! And is that a yorner in the corner?!" Expand the hunt further if you are having fun and go outside. Point up the tree and exclaim, "There's a glee up our tree! I see a lound on the ground!" Encourage, but don't demand, your child to tell what he or she sees.

✦ **Poetry Partners:**   "The Wendigo," "Slithergadee," "Eletelephony," "Gumble," "The Bluffalo," "The Little Man," and "Wrimples" from *The Random House Book of Children's Poetry;* "Cuckoo!" from *The New Kid on the Block.*

✦ **Related Books:**   Other books by Dr. Seuss are *One Fish, Two Fish, Red Fish, Blue Fish; The Cat in the Hat; The Cat in the Hat Comes Back; Fox in Socks; Green Eggs and Ham;* and *Horton Hears a Who!*

Book Share 49

*I like being around books. It makes me feel civilized.
The only way to do all the things you'd like to do
is read.*
— Tom Clancy

Title: *Eight Days of Hanukkah*

Author: Harriet Ziefert

Illustrator: Melinda Levine

Publisher: Viking

Summary: This simple, colorful book provides information about the eight days of Hanukkah on each of its eight pages. Rhyme is used to describe Hanukkah traditions such as lighting candles, frying latkes, giving gifts, singing songs, and spinning dreidels. Each page concludes the same way with "Do you know the reason why? It's Hanukkah tonight."

Key: Personal Value: Hanukkah

✦ **Setting and Materials Needed:** This book may be read before a meal or snack. You will need the ingredients listed below for making latkes (potato pancakes).

✦ **Before Reading Activity:** If you celebrate Hanukkah, tell your child that this book tells about some familiar holiday traditions. If your family does not celebrate Hanukkah, tell your child that you are going to read a book about a special holiday that is celebrated by many people in the world.

✦ **During Reading Activity:** Take advantage of the repetition on each page to elicit participation from your child. After you have read, "Do you know the reason why? It's Hanukkah tonight" at the end of each of several pages, encourage your child to answer with you, "It's Hanukkah tonight," throughout the remainder of the book.

Reread the book and ask your child to count how many candles appear on each page as you read. Before you count, tell (or remind) your child that the candle in the middle is the "helper" candle that lights each of the others throughout the eight-day period. As you turn from page to page, your child will see that the number of candles (not counting the helper candle) increases from one to eight. Notice the increase in the number of candles decorating the border of each page, too.

✦ **After Reading Activity:** This would be a wonderful time to make latkes together as part of a meal or as a snack. Return to the page that shows Grandmother making the latkes. Tell your child that this is a traditional Jewish food that is often made during the Hanukkah holiday. Then make your own. If you have never made them before, follow the recipe below. Otherwise, use your own recipe.

> *Latkes (Potato Pancakes)*
>
> 3 large potatoes
> 1 small onion
> 2 eggs
> 2 tablespoons of flour
> 1 teaspoon of salt
> pinch of pepper
> 1/2 cup of vegetable oil

Grate the unpeeled potatoes and onions coarsely, and combine in a bowl. Beat the eggs, and add them to the bowl. Add flour, salt, and pepper. Let the mixture thicken for ten minutes; then pour off the excess liquid. Heat the vegetable oil in a frying pan, then drop tablespoonfuls of the mixture into the pan. Turn once they are brown around the edges. Fry on the other side until golden brown. Drain on paper towels and eat! You may wish to add sour cream or applesauce.

✦ **Poetry Partners:** "Light the Festive Candles," "I Heard a Bird Sing," "Dreams," and "To Dark Eyes Dreaming" in *The Random House Book of Poetry for Children;* three Mother Goose poems about candles are "Jack," "Candle-Saving," and "A Candle" in *The Real Mother Goose.*

✦ **Related Books:** *Celebrate: A Book of Jewish Holidays* by Judith Gross; *Grandma's Latkes* by Malka Drucker; *My First Hanukkah Book* by Aileen L. Fisher; *Hershel and the Hanukkah Goblins* by Eric Kimmel; *Latkes and Applesauce* by Fran Manushkin; *Just Enough Is Plenty* by Barbara D. Goldin.

Book Share 50

The book is the vessel that contains all the ideas that are good and important in our culture. As such it must be cherished, preserved, and protected.
   —Andrew Ross

Title: *K Is for Kwanzaa*

Author: Juwanda G. Ford

Illustrator: Ken Wilson-Max

Publisher: Cartwheel

Summary: Kwanzaa is a seven-day nonreligious holiday that honors African Americans and their heritage. This alphabet book teaches the reader and listener much about the celebration.

Key: Alphabet

✦ **Setting and Materials Needed:** Oware, also known as mancala, is an African game played with marbles or small stones. Many young children enjoy this popular game, and you can find it at many local toy stores.

✦ **Before Reading Activity:** Teach your child to play mancala. Don't be rigid about following the rules if your child finds them frustrating. Allow your child to handle and manipulate the colorful stones and make up rules of his or her own! The idea is to have fun. Explain that this game originated in Africa, and point out Africa on a map or globe. After you have enjoyed the game, tell your child that the book you want to share is about a celebration called Kwanzaa that many people (possibly you) enjoy during December. Mancala is often played during Kwanzaa.

✦ **During Reading Activity:** Read the book. Talk about several of the pages. What activities that are similar to those in the book does your family do? For example, on the page "F is for feast," if you do not celebrate Kwanzaa, do you celebrate a different holiday with a feast? On the pages that discuss traditional Kwanzaa foods, talk about the special foods you eat during the holidays you celebrate.

✦ **After Reading Activity:** "T is for tales." The author explains that telling African tales is a popular Kwanzaa activity. Use this time to tell your child a tale. This might be a story from your childhood, a story that you have read, or something that you invent. Let your child tell you a story. Storytelling is a wonderful tradition and helps develop oral language as well as listening skills.

✦ **Poetry Partners:** "No Difference," "Helping," "The Little Blue Engine," and "Listen to the Mustn'ts" in *Where the Sidewalk Ends*; "The Clock" and "If All the Seas Were One Sea" in *The Real Mother Goose*; "Dreams" in *The Random House Book of Poetry for Children*.

✦ **Related Books:** *Anansi the Spider: A Tale from the Ashanti* by Gerald McDermott; *Anansi and the Talking Melon, Anansi and the Moss-Covered Rock,* and *Anansi Goes Fishing,* all by Eric Kimmel; *Seven Days of Kwanzaa* by Ella Grier; and *Ashanti to Zulu: African Traditions* by Margaret Musgrove.

Book Share 51

When I am reading a book, whether wise or silly,
it seems to be alive and talking to me.
  —Jonathan Swift

Title: *Chicken Soup with Rice*

Author: Maurice Sendak

Publisher: Scholastic

Summary: Maurice Sendak obviously enjoys chicken soup. For each month of the year, he writes a poem honoring this tasty concoction. In January it's nice to sip hot chicken soup with rice. In March the wind spills the soup, laps it up, and roars for more! This is a great book to read at the beginning of every month to see how chicken soup with rice is enjoyed throughout the year.

Key: Predictable and Pattern

✦ **Setting and Materials Needed:** The book sharing should take place at the kitchen or dining room table. You will be eating chicken soup with rice during the activity so you will need a can or container of the soup. You will also need plain paper and a writing instrument.

✦ **Before Reading Activity:** This activity would take place best over the noon meal. As you heat the chicken soup with rice say, "I wonder what is in this soup that makes it smell so good?" Read the label on the soup, "Oh, it says chicken soup with rice." Once the soup is heated, serve it and say, "I'm going to read you a book called *Chicken Soup with Rice*. I wonder why someone wrote a book about soup?"

✦ **During Reading Activity:** As you read the story and eat your soup, make a slight pause every time the refrain ". . . chicken soup with rice" is presented. Read the book a second time, and ask your son or daughter to make the statement (not with his or her mouth full!) "chicken soup with rice" each time you pause at the end of a month's poem. For example, at the end of the poem for the month of January, you read, "Sipping once, sipping twice, sipping . . . " (Pause and let your child finish with "chicken soup with rice!")

✦ **After Reading Activity:**   Say to your child, "Let's have some fun with this story. Let's think of some words that rhyme with rice and put them in the story *Chicken Soup with Rice*." Write *rice* down on a piece of paper and say, "I think mice and rice rhyme. What do you think?" Then read the story again saying mice in place of rice at each appropriate spot. Reading "chicken soup with mice" will present endless hilarity, if not to you, certainly to your child. Do the same thing with *ice*, *dice*, *lice*, and *nice*.

✦ **Poetry Partners:**   "If," "Pease Porridge," "Little Jack Horner," "Hot-Cross Buns," "Sing a Song of Sixpence," "The Cat and the Fiddle," and "Bat, Bat" in *The Real Mother Goose.*

✦ **Related Books:**   *Mouse Soup* by Arnold Lobel; *Alphabites: A Funny Feast from A to Z* by Charles Reasoner; *The Hungry Little Boy* by Joan W. Blos; and *Lunch* by Denise Fleming. Other favorite books by Maurice Sendak are *Where the Wild Things Are* and *In the Night Kitchen.*

Book Share 52

A book—a well composed book—is a magic carpet
on which we are wafted to a world we cannot enter
in any other way.
　　—Caroline Gordon

Title: *The Polar Express*

Author: Chris Van Allsburg

Publisher: Houghton Mifflin

Summary: A young boy lies in his bed one Christmas Eve, listening for the sounds of Santa's sleigh. Instead of sleigh bells, he hears hissing steam and squeaking metal. He peers out the window to see a train and is welcomed aboard the Polar Express, which takes him, along with many other children, to the North Pole and Santa. All of Santa's elves are gathered in the center of the city to watch Santa give the first gift of Christmas. The lucky boy is chosen to receive the first gift, and he asks for one of the bells from Santa's sleigh. When the boy gets back aboard the Polar Express, he discovers that the sleigh bell has slipped through a hole in his pocket and is gone. He finds the bell under his Christmas tree the next morning, with a note from Santa suggesting that he fix the hole in his pocket. Sadly, his parents cannot hear the beautiful sound the bell makes. Over the years, the bell falls silent for his friends—for only those who truly believe continue to hear its sound. This book is a must-read for anyone who believes in the magic of this holiday as well as for those who appreciate a well-told story and beautiful illustrations, whether or not they celebrate Christmas.

Key: Personal Value: Christmas

✦ **Setting and Materials Needed:** If you celebrate Christmas, this is a wonderful book to read on Christmas Eve when you are snuggled in a favorite chair with your child at the end of the day. A cup of hot chocolate will help set the mood. You may want to purchase a small silver sleigh bell to use after reading.

✦ **Before Reading Activity:**   Explain that Christmas is a holiday celebrated by many people around the world. Briefly talk about your family's customs and traditions, if any, surrounding this holiday.

✦ **During Reading Activity:**   Take your time reading this book so that you and your child can enjoy the beautiful illustrations.

✦ **After Reading Activity:**   Sit quietly and listen for the sound of Santa's sleigh. If you have a bell, listen to the sound it makes. If you celebrate Christmas, this would be a good time to set cookies and milk on the table for Santa. Then, let your child dictate to you a letter for Santa, thanking him in advance for any gifts he will deliver and bidding him a safe trip. Leave this letter next to the cookies.

✦ **Poetry Partners:**   "A Visit From St. Nicholas," "Gift with the Wrappings Off," "Merry Christmas" from *The Random House Book of Poetry for Children*; "Forgotten Language" and "Santa and the Reindeer" from *Where the Sidewalk Ends*; and "Little Jack Horner" and "Christmas" from *The Real Mother Goose*.

✦ **Related Books:**   *I Spy Christmas: A Book of Picture Riddles* by Walter Wick and Jean Marzollo; *The Christmas Alphabet* by Robert Sabuda; *The Poky Little Puppy's First Christmas* by Justine Korman; *The Little Drummer Boy* by Ezra Jack Keats; *Nicky's Christmas Surprise* by Harriet Ziefert; and *The Littlest Angel* by Charles Tazewell.

Book Share 53

In a real sense, people who have read good literature
have lived more than people who cannot or will not read.
—S. I. Hayakawa

Title: *Miss Bindergarten Gets Ready for Kindergarten*

Author: Joseph Slate

Illustrator: Ashley Wolff

Publisher: Dutton Children's Books

Summary: This book taps many aspects of beginning literacy. It is arranged alphabetically, makes use of rhyme and alliteration, and has tremendous personal appeal for young children who are approaching their first day of kindergarten. The book shows what Miss Bindergarten, a teacher, does to get ready for kindergarten and also shows what her 26 soon-to-be students (from Adam the alligator to Zach the zebra) are doing to get ready. This positive book capitalizes on children's anticipation of school.

Key: Special Moments: Going to school; Phonemic Awareness; Alphabet

✦ **Setting and Materials Needed:** Read this book in any comfortable room.

✦ **Before Reading Activity:** Without showing the book, engage your child in a conversation about school. Discuss the things you will need to do to get ready for school the morning of the first day. Talk also about what the teacher might be doing to get ready for kindergarten. Then get the book and say, "Here is a book about how a teacher and some children get ready for kindergarten. It's called *Miss Bindergarten Gets Ready for Kindergarten*."

✦ **During Reading Activity:** Read the entire story once uninterrupted, taking time to examine the pictures. Then go back and read it again. This time talk about what you see Miss Bindergarten doing to get ready for school. If your child has preschool experience, you might point out familiar aspects of Miss Bindergarten's classroom. When you have done this, go back again, and follow the alphabet through the book. Flip through the pages in order and say, "Look, Adam starts with A, Brenda starts with B, Christopher starts with C," and so on. If your child is interested in one more read through, ask him or her to use the pictures as clues to the rhymes and to try to participate in reading the story with you. Then as you read, pause before the rhyme "Brenda Heath brushes her (pause) teeth." "Jessie Sike pedals her (pause) bike."

✦ **After Reading Activity:** Talk to your child about going to kindergarten. Ask your child what he or she thinks it will be like. Use this as an opportunity to talk about fears, misconceptions, and positive expectations.

You may wish to write a list of the things that you will need to do to get ready. As you complete them, check them off on the list.

✦ **Poetry Partners:** "The Creature in the Classroom," "The Marrog," "Wiggly Giggles," "Alley Cat School," "The Wrong Start," and "Follow the Leader" in *The Random House Book of Poetry for Children* and "The Mulberry Bush" in *The Real Mother Goose.*

✦ **Related Books:** *Spot Goes to School* by Eric Hill; *The Berenstain Bears Go to School* by Stan and Jan Berenstain; *Lilly's Purple Plastic Purse* by Kevin Henkes; *Chrysanthemum* by Kevin Henkes; *The Kissing Hand* by Audrey Penn; *I Need a Lunch Box* by Jeannette Caines; and *Will I Have a Friend?* by Miriam Cohen.

Book Share 54

Nothing is pleasanter than exploring a library.
—Walter Savage Landor

Title: *This Is the Way We Go to School*

Author: Edith Baer

Illustrator: Steve Bjorkman

Publisher: Scholastic

Summary: Making use of rhyme, this book tells the many ways that children around the world travel to school. For instance, "Jenny, Jerry, Pete, and Perry ride the Staten Island Ferry" and "Bicycles bring Mei and Ling through the traffic of Nanjing." This is a wonderful book for building children's awareness of the similarities and differences of people around the world.

Key: Special Moments: Going to school; Phonemic Awareness

✦ **Setting and Materials Needed:** Read this book in any comfortable setting. Ideally, after reading the book you will take a trip to the school your child will attend as a preschooler or kindergartener. Reading midday on a weekend may make this most convenient.

✦ **Before Reading Activity:** Before reading, tell your child that this book is about the many ways children around the world travel to school, such as walking or riding in cars. Ask your child to think of some ways people might travel to school. See how many different ways you can think of together. Then tell your child to listen for whether the author wrote about these ways.

✦ **During Reading Activity:** As you read, talk about the pictures in the book. It is likely that there will be new vocabulary and concepts, and the pictures will support your child's understanding. Comment on those modes of transportation that the two of you have already thought about, and discuss those modes that you had not discussed before reading the book.

✦ **After Reading Activity:** After reading the story, talk about how your child will travel to school when the time comes. Which children in the story is your child most like in this way? Take this opportunity to go by your child's school—drive, walk, ride your bikes, take a bus. If you have not done so yet, you may want to walk around the school (when it is not in session), and let your child play on the playground. A sense of familiarity with the school makes the first day of school a more positive experience.

✦ **Poetry Partners:** "Sing a Song of Subways," "Sing a Song of People," "If Once You Have Slept on an Island," "Train Song," "Flight Plan," and "Routine" from *The Random House Book of Children's Poetry;* "This is the Way" from *The Real Mother Goose.*

✦ **Related Books:** *Hopscotch Around the World* and *Jacks Around the World* both by Mary D. Lankford; *This Is My House* by Arthur Dorros; *Bread Bread Bread, Hats Hats Hats,* and *Shoes Shoes Shoes,* all by Ann Morris.

Book Share 55

The world exists to be put in a book.
—Stephane Mallarme

Title: *A Birthday for Frances*

Author: Russell Hoban

Illustrator: Lillian Hoban

Publisher: HarperTrophy

Summary: Frances is an endearing little badger who has difficulty dealing with the fact that tomorrow is her little sister's birthday. When the day arrives, however, she sings "Happy Birthday" to her sister and gives her a coveted Chompo Bar.

Key: Special Moments: Birthday

✦ **Setting and Materials Needed:** Read this book at the end of the day on your child's birthday. Have note cards and a pen available for the after reading activity.

✦ **Before Reading Activity:** Spend some time reflecting on the day. Talk about the special activities your child engaged in and how much fun you had. Tell your child that you are going to share a book about a little badger named Frances whose sister has a birthday. Do a "picture walk" through the story before reading it. Look at the pictures, and talk about what is happening. What are the family members doing? How does Frances's family celebrate birthdays? Can your child figure out what gift Frances gives her sister?

✦ **During Reading Activity:** Enjoy the book. Point to the word "Chompo" on the candy bar when Frances carries it home. Ask your child if it sounds like a good chocolate bar.

✦ **After Reading Activity:** Ask your child what he or she thought of the book. If it is appropriate, you might want to talk about the fact that for some children it is hard to watch others get attention and receive gifts.

Have your child help you write a list of the gifts he or she received today. Then, as your child dictates, write thank you notes to the people who gave him or her the gifts.

✦ **Poetry Partners:** "Happy Birthday, Dear Dragon" and "I'm Disgusted with My Brother" from *New Kid on the Block*; "A Week of Birthdays" from *The Real Mother Goose*; "Surprises," "If We Didn't Have Birthdays," "I Am Me," and "Just Me" from *The Random House Book of Poetry for Children*.

✦ **Related Books:** *Happy Birthday, Ronald Morgan!* by Patricia Reilly Giff; *Clifford's Birthday Party* by Norman Bridwell; *Flower Garden* by Eve Bunting; and *On the Day You Were Born* by Debra Frasier all make good birthday reading. Two excellent adoption stories are *Tell Me Again About the Night I Was Born* by Jamie Lee Curtis and *Over the Moon: An Adoption Tale* by Karen Katz.

Book Share 56

Readers are lucky—they will never be bored or lonely.
—Natalie Babbit

Title: *The Berenstain Bears' Moving Day*

Authors: Stan and Jan Berenstain

Publisher: Random House

Summary: The Bear family lives in a hillside cave at the edge of Bear Country, but they have outgrown their home and now it is time to move. Brother Bear is concerned about his toys, books, and friends. Mama and Papa assure him that they will take all of his belongings with them to the new house. As for his friends, they can write and visit, but Brother Bear will make new friends in his new neighborhood. Brother spends a night worrying about his move. The next day, the movers pack all of the Bears' belongings, the Bears say good-bye to their friends, and they drive into the valley to their new home. Soon they are greeted by many friendly neighbors welcoming them to the neighborhood. That night Brother Bear goes to sleep very happy.

Key: Special Moments: Moving to a new home

✦ **Setting and Materials Needed:** Read this book before you move into a new home or neighborhood. It is most appropriate for daytime reading. You will want to have available packing boxes or bags so your child can assist in this big moment in his or her life.

✦ **Before Reading Activity:** Talk to your child about your upcoming move. Explain that many people move and that you want to share a story about moving.

✦ **During Reading Activity:** Read the book.

✦ **After Reading Activity:** Talk about how Brother Bear felt before and after his move. Assist your child in packing some of his or her belongings for your move. It will give your child peace of mind that treasured possessions will not be left behind, and participating in the process is important. Label the boxes (for example, "Carmela's toys," "Carmela's books"). Reassure your child that you can write or visit old friends, and give him or her pieces of paper with your new address written on them to distribute to friends. Take a picture of your child in front of your old and your new house.

✦ **Poetry Partners:** "Since Hanna Moved Away," "Home! You're Where It's Warm Inside," "The Folk Who Live in Backward Town," and "Our House" from *The Random House of Poetry for Children*; "The Neighbors Are Not Fond of Me" from *The New Kid on the Block*; and "The House That Jack Built" from *The Real Mother Goose*.

✦ **Related Books:** *Goodbye House* by Frank Asch; *Ira Says Goodbye* by Bernard Waber; *Andrew Jessup* by Nette Hilton; *Alexander, Who's Not (Do You Hear Me? I Mean It!) Going to Move* by Judith Viorst; and *We Are Best Friends* and *Best Friends Together Again* by Aliki.

Book Share 57

Reading is the sole means by which we slip, involuntarily, often helplessly, into another's skin, another's voice, another's soul.
—Joyce Carol Oates

Title: *Curious George Goes to the Hospital*

Authors: Margret and H. A. Rey

Publisher: Houghton Mifflin

Summary: Curious George, a monkey, has to take a trip to the hospital after he swallows a puzzle piece. He talks to a nurse and doctor, has an x-ray taken, and is scheduled for surgery. When he is admitted to the hospital and taken to the children's ward, he sees several other children with various ailments. He is frightened but gets through the surgery just fine. As he is recovering, Curious George, up to his usual antics, disrupts a tour that the mayor is taking and succeeds in making a very sad and frightened little girl laugh.

Key: Special Moments: Going to the hospital

✦ **Setting and Materials Needed:** When and where you choose to read this book depends on the circumstances. Your child may make a scheduled visit to the hospital (as Curious George does), may have a friend or relative in the hospital, or may make an emergency trip to the doctor or hospital. This will influence whether you read the book before, during, or after the visit.

✦ **Before Reading Activity:** Tell your child that you would like to share a book about a little monkey that must go to the hospital. Ask your child how he or she thinks the monkey feels about going to the hospital. Acknowledge that it can be an interesting adventure, but that it can also be a bit scary.

✦ **During Reading Activity:** Read the book and point out any similarities that you know will exist between Curious George's adventure and that of your child. Comment on how friendly and helpful the hospital staff in the book are.

✦ **After Reading Activity:**   In this book, children are in the hospital for a variety of reasons. Talk about those reasons and about people you know who have been in the hospital. Pretend that you and your child are two doctors and "treat" a stuffed animal. Imagine it needs surgery and act out the process from admission to release from the hospital. If your child has a broken limb, you might wrap the toy's arm or leg in a bandage.

✦ **Poetry Partners:**   "Crocodile's Toothache," "Sick," and "Band-aids" from *Where the Sidewalk Ends*; "Doctor Fell" in *The Real Mother Goose*; "Wendy in Winter" in *The Random House Book of Poetry for Children*; and "I've Got an Incredible Headache" and "Nine Mice" in *The New Kid on the Block*.

✦ **Related Books:**   Other books with a medical theme include *Madeline* by Ludwig Bemelmans; *I'm Going to the Doctor* by Kathryn Siegler; *A Visit to the Sesame Street Hospital* by Can Elliott and Deborah Hautzig; and *Stitches* by Harriet Ziefert. Two additional Curious George books are *Curious George* and *Curious George Learns the Alphabet* by Margret and H. A. Rey.

Book Share 58

A book is magical; it transcends time and space.
—Daniel J. Boorstin

Title: *The New Baby*

Author: Mercer Mayer

Publisher: Golden

Summary: We especially like this book because it presents such a positive view of a new baby in the family, unlike some books that emphasize an older sibling's jealousy of the attention a new baby receives. When the new baby comes home, Critter takes out all of his favorite toys and games to show his baby sister. He tells her jokes. She does not pay attention. What can you do with a new baby, he wonders. Soon Critter learns how to cuddle with her, tickle her, and play in appropriate ways with her. The book ends with Critter showing off his new sister to his friends and announcing, "They think I'm so lucky."

Key: Special Moments: New baby

✦ **Setting and Materials Needed:** A favorite old chair where the two of you can cuddle will be a perfect setting. Have a photo album (or loose photos) of your child when he or she was a newborn ready for the before reading activity. Use a baby doll, teddy bear, or other stuffed animal for the after reading activity.

✦ **Before Reading Activity:** Before reading this book, show your child photos of when he or she was a newborn. Talk about the day he or she was born, what a special day it was, and how special he or she is.

✦ **During Reading Activity:** Read the book. Take a minute to talk about the ways that Critter is learning to play with his new sister.

✦ **After Reading Activity:** Using a teddy bear or doll, teach your child how to hold a baby, rock it, give it a bottle, and change its diaper. If it can be immersed in water, let your child help you give the doll a bath. Have your child dictate a list of the things that he or she wants to do someday with his or her new sibling. Talking and writing about these ideas serves the dual purposes of helping to prepare your child for a new member of the family and having a record of his or her ideas for future enjoyment.

✦ **Poetry Partners:** "What a Day" and "For Sale" from *Where the Sidewalk Ends;* "Six Weeks Old" from *The Random House Book of Poetry for Children;* "My Baby Brother" from *New Kid on the Block;* "Bye, Baby Bunting," "Rock-a-Bye, Baby," and "Dance, Little Boy" from *The Real Mother Goose.*

✦ **Related Books:** *Arthur's Baby* by Marc Brown; *Berenstain Bears' New Baby* by Stan and Jan Berenstain; *The Crane Girl* by Veronika Martenova Charles; *Peter's Chair* by Ezra Jack Keats; *Welcoming Babies* by Margy Burns Knight; and *Welcome, Little Baby* by Aliki.

Book Share 59

A wonderful thing about a book, in contrast to a computer screen, is that you can take it to bed with you.

    —Daniel J. Boorstin

Title: *Ira Sleeps Over*

Author: Bernard Waber

Publisher: Houghton Mifflin

Summary: Young Ira is very excited when his friend Reggie invites him to his first sleepover—until Ira's sister asks if he is going to take his teddy bear along. Ira replies, "Of course not!" but then his sister reminds him that he has never slept without his teddy bear before. Thus begins Ira's struggle with deciding whether to take his teddy bear. His sister, ever present with her comments, adds to his struggle. In this humorous and tender story, we witness a boy make an important decision as he prepares for a big event in his young life.

Key: Special Moments: Sleeping over

✦ **Setting and Materials Needed:** Your child's bedroom would make a good setting for reading aloud this book. Have a suitcase or backpack ready for packing, and be sure your child's teddy bear (or other favorite bedtime comfort, such as a blanket) is nearby.

✦ **Before Reading Activity:** If you have selected this book because your child is going to a sleepover, begin by asking your child what things he or she would like to take. Get out a backpack or suitcase, and pack it with pajamas, toothbrush and toothpaste, and other items. Let your child participate in the decision making and packing. If your child does not select a teddy bear or other stuffed animal, ask if he or she would like to take a favorite stuffed animal. Then, tell your child you are going to read a book about a boy named Ira who has been invited to his very first sleepover and has some decisions of his own to make about what to bring and what to leave behind. (If you think your child will be highly influenced by Ira's concerns about his friend's reaction to his teddy bear, you may wish to save the reading of the book until after your child returns from the sleepover.)

✦ **During Reading Activity:** Put your child's teddy bear near enough for your child to reach over and hold it. At each point during the story when Ira decides to take his teddy bear, encourage your child to hold the bear. At each point in the story when Ira decides not to take his teddy bear, have your child set the teddy bear aside. Hopefully, your child will have fun picking the bear up and setting it down multiple times throughout the story! At several points, ask your child to predict what Ira's decision will be. For instance, when Ira's sister asks what Ira will do if Reggie wants to know the teddy bear's name, read "I decided . . . " (pause here or say "What do you think he decided now?") "NOT to take my teddy bear." Laugh together at Ira's frequent change of mind.

✦ **After Reading Activity:** Talk about all of the things that Ira and Reggie did at Reggie's house. Then, talk about all the things your child hopes to do at his or her friend's house (or, if the sleepover has already occurred, talk about what things they did). If your child is interested, help write his or her own sleepover book, "(Your child's name) Sleeps Over." Let your child dictate to you a few sentences that tell about his or her sleepover. Illustrate your child's sleepover book together.

✦ **Poetry Partners:** "From: The Bed Book" and "Wrestling" in *The Random House Book of Poetry for Children;* "Hug o' War" and "For Sale" in *Where the Sidewalk Ends;* "Mean Maxine" and "Oh, Teddy Bear" in *The New Kid on the Block;* "Bedtime" in *The Real Mother Goose.*

✦ **Related Books:** *Spot Sleeps Over* by Eric Hill; *My Best Friend* by Pat Hutchins; *The Berenstain Bears and the Slumber Party* by Stan and Jan Berenstain; *Pajama Party* by Amy Hest; *Franklin Has a Sleepover* by Paulette Bourgeois; and also by Bernard Waber, *Lyle, Lyle, Crocodile.*

Book Share 60

It is a great thing to start life with a small number of really good books which are your very own.
—Sir Arthur Conan Doyle

Title: *Who Wants Arthur?*

Author: Amanda Graham

Illustrator: Donna Gynell

Publisher: Gareth Stevens

Summary: Arthur is an ordinary dog who lives in Mrs. Humber's Pet Shop. He desperately wants a home but just can't seem to get any customers interested in him. On Monday, all the customers want rabbits. Monday night Arthur practices being a rabbit—he eats carrots, pokes out his front teeth, and makes his ears stand up straight. The next day, everybody wants snakes; nobody wants a dog who acts like a rabbit. So that night Arthur practices being a snake, but again nobody purchases him. By the end of the week, Arthur has tried being a rabbit, a snake, a fish, a cat, a frog, a mouse, and a parakeet. Then a little girl enters the store with her grandpa. They ask the owner to see the very special dog who performs tricks. When the girl sees Arthur, she picks him up and hugs him. Arthur happily gives her the biggest, wettest, doggiest lick ever. He has found a home.

Key: Special Moments: New pet

✦ **Setting and Materials Needed:** Read this book near your new pet. A camera or drawing paper and crayons will be needed for the after reading activity.

✦ **Before Reading Activity:** Talk with your child about your new pet. Why did you choose it? Look at your pet, and talk about what makes it special. Tell your child that you are going to read a book about a dog who desperately wants to become someone's pet.

✦ **During Reading Activity:** Once your child recognizes the predictable pattern of this book (that is, that each evening Arthur practices behaving like the best-selling animal of the day), encourage him or her to predict what the animal will do each evening. What will Arthur practice tonight? Then you and your child practice behaving like each animal. Hop around the room, meow like a cat, swim like a fish, whatever is appropriate for the pet you are discussing.

✦ **After Reading Activity:** Take a photograph of your pet or let your child draw a picture of it. When you get the film developed, or after your child has drawn the picture, talk again about how special your pet is. Ask your child to dictate a sentence or two about your pet while you record it underneath the photograph or drawing. Tape the picture to your refrigerator!

✦ **Poetry Partners:** "Mother Doesn't Want a Dog," "The Hairy Dog," "Cats," "Cat's Menu," and "Mice" in *The Random House Book of Poetry for Children*; "Double-Tail Dog" in *Where the Sidewalk Ends*; and "My Dog, He Is an Ugly Dog" in *The New Kid on the Block*.

✦ **Related Books:** *Arthur's New Puppy* by Marc Brown; *Officer Buckle and Gloria* by Peggy Rathmann; *Henry and Mudge: The First Book of Their Adventures* by Cynthia Rylant; *Amigo* by Byrd Baylor; *Any Kind of Dog* by Lynn Reiser; and *Puppy Care and Critters, Too!* by Judy Petersen-Fleming and Bill Fleming.

References for Book Share Featured and Recommended Children's Books

Aardema, V. (1992). *Bringing the Rain to Kapiti Plain: A Nandi Tale*. New York: Dial Books for Young Readers.

Ahlberg, J. & A. (1979). *Each Peach Pear Plum*. New York: Viking.

Ahlberg, J. & A. (1991). *The Jolly Christmas Postman*. Boston: Little, Brown.

Ahlberg, J. & A. (1986). *The Jolly Postman*. Boston: Little, Brown.

Aliki. (1995). *Best Friends Together Again*. New York: Greenwillow.

Aliki. (1996). *Go Tell Aunt Rhody*. New York: Aladdin.

Aliki. (1992). *My Hands*. New York: HarperCollins.

Aliki. (1987). *We Are Best Friends*. New York: William Morrow.

Aliki. (1993). *Welcome Little Baby*. New York: William Morrow.

Anglund, J. W. (1997). *A Bedtime Book*. New York: Aladdin.

Anno, M. (1986). *Anno's Counting Book*. New York: HarperTrophy.

Aronsky, J. (1996). *Every Autumn Comes the Bear*. New York: Putnam.

Asch, F. (1989). *Goodbye House*. New York: Aladdin.

Asch, F. (1982). *Happy Birthday Moon*. New York: Aladdin.

Baer, E. (1992). *This Is the Way We Go to School*. New York: Scholastic.

Baker, A. (1994). *Gray Rabbit's 1, 2, 3*. Fredericton, New Brunswick: Kingfisher.

Baker, A. (1994). *Black and White Rabbit's ABC*. Fredericton, New Brunswick: Kingfisher.

Baker, A. (1994). *Brown Rabbit's Shape Book*. Fredericton, New Brunswick: Kingfisher.

Baker, A. (1994). *White Rabbit's Color Book*. Fredericton, New Brunswick: Kingfisher.

Bancroft, H., & Van Gelder, R. G. (1997). *Animals in Winter*. New York: HarperTrophy.

Barrett, J. (1989). *Animals Should Definitely Not Act Like People*. New York: Aladdin.

Barrett, J. (1989). *Animals Should Definitely Not Wear Clothing*. New York: Aladdin.

Barrett, J. (1985). *Cloudy with a Chance of Meatballs*. New York: Live Oak Media.

Barton, B. (1990). *Building a House*. New York: Mulberry.

Bayer, J. (1992). *A My Name Is Alice*. New York: E. P. Dutton.

Baylor, B. (1989). *Amigo*. New York: Aladdin.

Baylor, B. (1987). *The Desert Is Theirs*. New York: Aladdin.

Baylor, B. (1987). *Everyone Needs a Rock*. New York: Aladdin.

Baylor, B. (1986). *Hawk, I'm Your Brother*. New York: Aladdin.

Baylor, B. (1986). *I'm in Charge of Celebrations*. New York: Atheneum.

Baylor, B. (1984). *If You Are a Hunter of Fossils*. New York: Aladdin.

Baylor, B. (1982). *Moon Song*. New York: Scribner's.

Becken, J. (1991). *Seven Little Rabbits*. New York: Scholastic.

Bemelmans, L. (1977). *Madeline*. New York: Viking.

Berenstain, S. & J. (1981). *The Berenstain Bears' Moving Day*. New York: Random House.

Berenstain, S. & J. (1974). *Berenstain Bears' New Baby*. New York: Random House.

Berenstain, S. & J. (1990). *The Berenstain Bears and the Slumber Party* . New York: Random House.

Berenstain, S. & J. (1989). *The Berenstain Bears and Too Much TV*. New York: Random House.

Blos, J. (1998). *One Very Best Valentine's Day*. New York: Aladdin.

Blos, J. W. (1995). *The Hungry Little Boy*. New York: Simon & Schuster.

Bond, F. (1990). *Four Valentines in a Rainstorm*. New York: HarperTrophy.

Bond, M. (1992). *Paddington at the Seashore*. New York: Harper Festival.

Bond, M. (1992). *Paddington Takes a Bath*. New York: Harper Festival.

Bourgeois, P. (1992). *Franklin Has a Sleepover*. New York: Scholastic.

Boynton, S. (1987). *A Is for Angry*. New York: Workman.

Boynton, S. (1996). *Hippos Go Berserk*. New York: Aladdin.

Branley, F. (1997). *Down Comes the Rain*. New York: HarperTrophy.

Brett, J. (1997). *The Hat*. New York: Putnam.

Brett, J. (1996). *The Mitten*. New York: Putnam.

Bridwell, N. (1990). *Clifford's Birthday Party*. New York: Scholastic.

Bridwell, N. (1991). *Clifford's Halloween*. New York: Scholastic.

Bridwell, N. (1988). *Clifford, the Big Red Dog*. New York: Scholastic.

Bridwell, N. (1990). *Clifford's ABC*. New York: Scholastic.

Bridwell, N. (1991). *The Witch Next Door*. New York: Scholastic.

Briggs, R. (1994). *The Bear*. New York: Random Library.

Brinckloe, J. (1986). *Fireflies!* Newyork: Aladdin.

Brown, M. (1990). *Arthur's Baby*. Boston: Joy St. Books.

Brown, M. (1991). *Arthur's Birthday*. Boston: Little, Brown.

Brown, M. (1995). *Arthur's New Puppy*. Boston: Little, Brown.

Brown, M. (1993). *Arthur's Pet Business*. Boston: Little, Brown.

Brown, M. (1987). *Stone Soup*. New York: Aladdin.

Brown, M. W. (1991). *Goodnight Moon*. New York: Harper.

Brown, M. W. (1998). *The Runaway Bunny*. New York: Harper.

Brown, T. (1995). *Someone Special, Just Like You*. New York: Owlet.

Buchanan, K., & Buchanan, D. (1994). *It Rained on the Desert Today*. Flagstaff, AZ: Rising Moon.

Bunting, E. (1994). *Flower Garden*. New York: Harcourt Brace.

Bunting, E. (1985). *The Valentine Bears*. New York: Clarion.

Caines, J. (1993). *I Need a Lunch Box*. New York: HarperTrophy.

Carle, E. (1996). *1, 2, 3, to the Zoo*. New York: Philomel.

Carle, E. (1988). *Do You Want to Be My Friend?* New York: Putnam.

Carle, E. (1998). *Draw Me a Star*. New York: Paper Star.

Carle, E. (1996). *The Grouchy Ladybug*. New York: Crowell.

Carle, E. (1988). *The Mixed-Up Chameleon*. New York: Crowell.

Carle, E. (1987). *The Tiny Seed*. New York: Simon & Schuster.

Carle, E. (1985). *The Very Busy Spider*. New York: Philomel.

Carle, E. (1986). *The Very Hungry Caterpillar*. New York: Putnam.

Carle, E. (1995). *The Very Lonely Firefly*. New York: Putnam.

Carle, E. (1997). *The Very Quiet Cricket*. New York: Putnam.

Carlson, N. (1996). *Louanne Pig in the Mysterious Valentine*. Minneapolis: Carolrhoda.

Carlstrom, N. W. (1996). *Jesse Bear, What Will You Wear?* New York: Aladdin.

Charles, V. M. (1997). *The Crane Girl*. Buffalo, NY: Stoddart Kids.

Chorao, K. (1984). *The Baby's Bedtime Book*. New York: Puffin.

Christelow, E. (1996). *Don't Wake Up Mama*. New York: Clarion.

Christelow, E. (1991). *Five Little Monkeys Jumping on the Bed*. New York: Clarion.

Christelow, E. (1993). *Five Little Monkeys Sitting in a Tree*. New York: Clarion.

Cohen, M. (1989). *Will I Have a Friend?* New York: Aladdin.

Crowe, R., & Chorao, K. (1993). *Clyde Monster*. New York: E. P. Dutton.

Curtis, J. L. (1996). *Tell Me Again About the Day I Was Born*. New York: HarperCollins.

DePaola, T. (1997). *The Art Lesson*. New York: Paper Star.

DePaola, T. (1984). *The Popcorn Book*. New York: Holiday House.

De Regniers, B. S. (1997). *What Can You Do with a Shoe?* Tappan, NJ: Margaret McElderry.

De Regniers, B. S. (1989). *May I Bring a Friend?* New York: Aladdin.

Demi. (1996). *The Empty Pot*. New York: Holt.

Dobrin, A. J. (1992). *Josephine's 'magination*. New York: Scholastic.

Dorros, A. (1992). *This Is My House*. New York: Scholastic.

Drucker, M. (1996). *Grandma's Latkes*. New York: Harcourt Brace.

Eastman, P. D. (1988). *Are You My Mother?* New York: Random House.

Eastman, P. D. (1988). *Sam and the Firefly*. New York: Random House.

Ehlert, L. (1997). *Color Farm*. New York: HarperCollins.

Ehlert, L. (1997). *Color Zoo*. New York: HarperCollins.

Ehlert, L. (1992). *Fish Eyes: A Book You Can Count On*. New York: Harcourt Brace.

Ehrlich, D. (1988). *Animal Alphabet*. Wheeling, IL: National School Services.

Elliot, D., & Hautzig, D. (1985). *A Visit to the Sesame Street Hospital*. New York: Random House.

Fisher, A. L. (1985). *My First Hanukkah Book*. Chicago: Children's Press.

Fleming, D. (1997). *Barnyard Banter*. New York: Owlet.

Fleming, D. (1997). *Count*. New York: Holt.

Fleming, D. (1996). *Lunch*. New York: Holt.

Fleming, D. (1993). *In the Small, Small Pond*. New York: Holt.

Fleming, D. (1993). *In the Tall, Tall Grass*. New York: Owlet.

Ford, J. G. (1997). *K Is for Kwanzaa*. New York: Cartwheel.

Fox, M. (1994). *Koala Lou*. New York: Harcourt Brace.

Frasier, D. (1995). *On the Day You Were Born*. New York: Harcourt Brace.

Freeman, D. (1976). *Corduroy*. New York: Viking.

Freeman, D. (1997). *A Pocket for Corduroy*. New York: Puffin.

Gag, W. (1996). *Millions of Cats*. New York: Paper Star.

Galdone, P. (1984). *Henny Penny*. Boston: Houghton Mifflin.

Gauch, P. L. (1996). *Bravo, Tanya*. New York: Putnam.

Gauch, P. L. (1998). *Christina Katerina & the Box*. New York: Putnam.

Gauch, P. L. (1987). *Christina Katerina and the Time She Quit the Family*. New York: Putnam.

Gauch, P. L. (1989). *Dance, Tanya*. New York: Philomel.

Geisert, A. (1997). *The Etcher's Studio*. Boston: Houghton Mifflin.

George, T. (1989). *Box Turtle at Long Pond*. New York: Greenwillow.

Getty Museum (1997). *A Is for Artist: A Getty Museum Alphabet*. Los Angeles: Getty Museum.

Gibbons, G. (1991). *From Seed to Plant*. New York: Holiday House.

Gibbons, G. (1997). *The Moon Book*. New York: Holiday House.

Giff, P. R. (1988). *Happy Birthday, Ronald Morgan*. New York: Viking.

Gilks, H. (1993). *Bears*. New York: Ticknor & Fields.

Goldin, B. D. (1990). *Just Enough Is Plenty*. New York: Puffin.

Gomi, T. (1992). *Who Ate It?* Brookfield, PA: Millbrook.

Goode, D. (1996). *Mama's Perfect Present*. New York: Dutton Children's Books.

Graham, A. (1987). *Who Wants Arthur?* Milwaukee, WI: Gareth Stevens.

Greenway, S. (1992). *Whose Baby Am I? (Animals Q & A)*. Nashville, TN: Ideals Children's Books.

Grier, E. (1997). *Seven Days of Kwanzaa*. New York: Viking.

Grifalconi, A. (1986). *The Village of Round and Square Houses*. Boston: Brown.

Gross, J. (1992). *Celebrate: A Book of Jewish Holidays*. Los Angeles: Price Stern.

Guarino, D. (1991). *Is Your Mama a Llama?* New York: Scholastic.

Hanford, M. (1997). *Where's Waldo?* Cambridge, MA: Candlewick.

Harrison, D. L. (1997). *The Animal's Song*. Honesdale, PA: Boyds Mills.

Hawes, J. (1991). *Fireflies in the Night*. New York: Crowell.

Heiligman, D. (1996). *From Caterpillar to Butterfly*. New York: HarperTrophy.

Heller, R. (1995). *Color*. New York: Grosset & Dunlap.

Henkes, K. (1996). *Chrysanthemum*. New York: Mulberry Books.

Henkes, K. (1996). *Lily's Purple Plastic Purse*. New York: Greenwillow.

Hest, A. (1992). *Pajama Party*. New York: William Morrow.

Hill, E. (1984). *Spot Goes to School*. New York: Putnam.

Hill, E. (1996). *Spot Sleeps Over*. New York: Puffin.

Hilton, N. (1993). *Andrew Jessup*. New York: Ticknor & Fields.

Hoban, R. (1994). *Best Friends for Frances*. New York: HarperTrophy.

Hoban, R. (1994). *A Birthday for Frances*. New York: HarperTrophy.

Hoban, R. (1993). *Bread and Jam for Frances*. New York: HarperTrophy.

Hoban, T. (1993). *Black on White*. New York: Greenwillow.

Hoban, T. (1985). *1, 2, 3*. New York: William Morrow.

Hoban, T. (1995). *26 Letters and 99 Cents*. New York: Mulberry.

Hoban, T. (1993). *White on Black*. New York: Mulberry.

Hoff, S. (1985). *Who Will Be My Friends?* New York: HarperTrophy.

Howe, J. (1994). *I Wish I Were a Butterfly*. New York: Voyager.

Hurd, T. (1992). *Little Mouse's Big Valentine*. New York: HarperCollins.

Hutchins, P. (1989). *The Doorbell Rang*. New York: Mulberry.

Hutchins, P. (1993). *My Best Friend*. New York: Greenwillow.

Hutchins, P. (1983). *Rosie's Walk*. New York: Aladdin.

Isadora, R. (1992). *City Seen from A to Z*. New York: Mulberry.

Jenkins, P. B. (1995). *A Nest Full of Eggs*. New York: HarperTrophy.

Johnson, C. (1981). *Harold and the Purple Crayon*. New York: HarperTrophy.

Johnson, S. T. (1996). *Alphabet City*. New York: Viking.

Jones, C. (1998). *This Old Man*. Boston: Houghton Mifflin.

Joosse, B. M. (1991). *Mama, Do You Love Me?* San Francisco: Chronicle.

Jordan, H. (1992). *How a Seed Grows*. New York: HarperTrophy.

Jordan, T. (1996). *Amazon Alphabet*. Fredericton, New Brunswick: Kingfisher.

Kasza, K. (1996). *The Wolf's Chicken Stew*. New York: Paper Star.

Katz, K. (1997). *Over the Moon: An Adoption Tale*. New York: Holt.

Kaye, B., Wise, F., & Lippman, S. (1996). *A You're Adorable*. Cambridge, MA: Candlewick.

Keats, E. J. (1985). *Jeannie's Hat*. New York: HarperTrophy.

Keats, E. J. (1987). *The Little Drummer Boy*. New York: Aladdin.

Keats, E. J. (1991). *Over in the Meadow*. New York: Scholastic.

Keats, E. J. (1985). *Peter's Chair*. New York: HarperCollins.

Keats, E. J. (1981). *The Snowy Day*. New York: Viking.

Kimmel, E. (1993). *Anansi Goes Fishing*. New York: Holiday House.

Kimmel, E. (1994). *Hershel and the Hanukkah Goblins*. New York: Holiday House.

Kimmel, E. (1990). *Anansi and the Moss-Covered Rock*. New York: Holiday House.

Kimmel, E. (1995). *Anansi and the Talking Melon*. New York: Holiday House.

Knight, M. B. (1997). *Welcoming Babies*. Gardiner, ME: Tilbury House.

Korman, J. (1997). *The Poky Little Puppy's First Christmas*. New York: Golden.

Krauss, R. (1989). *The Carrot Seed*. New York: HarperTrophy.

Krauss, R. (1989). *The Happy Day*. New York: HarperTrophy.

Krauss, R. (1989). *A Hole Is To Dig: A First Book of First Definitions*. New York: HarperTrophy.

Krauss, R. (1973). *I'll Be You and You Be Me*. Freeport, ME: Bookstore Press.

Krauss, R. (1998). *My Little Library*. New York: HarperCollins.

Krauss, R. (1990). *Somebody Else's Nut Tree and Other Tales from Children*. North Haven, CT: Linnet.

Krauss, R. (1953). *A Very Special House*. New York: Harper Crest.

Kreeger, C. (1991). *Alaska ABC Book*. Homer, AK: Paws IV.

Lankford, M. D. (1996). *Hopscotch around the World*. New York: Beech Tree.

Lankford, M. D. (1996). *Jacks around the World*. New York: William Morrow.

Lear, E. (1992). *A Book of Nonsense*. New York: Everyman's Library.

Lear, E. (1997). *A Was Once an Apple Pie*. Cambridge, MA: Candlewick.

Lear, E. (1992). *Daffy Down Dillies: Silly Limericks*. Honesdale, PA: Boyds Mills.

Lear, E. (1994). *How Pleasant to Know Mr. Lear: Nonsense Poems*. Owings Mill, MD: Stemmer House.

Lear, E. (1997). *The Owl and the Pussycat*. Cambridge, MA: Candlewick.

Lear, E. (1995). *The Pelican Chorus and Other Nonsense*. New York: Harper Crest.

Lear, E. (1997). *The Quangle Wangle's Hat*. New York: Voyager.

Ling, M. (1992). *Owl (See How They Grow)*. La Vergne, TN: Dk Publishing.

Lionni, L. (1990). *The Apple Tree*. New York: Knopf.

Lionni, L. (1987). *Frederick*. New York: Knopf.

Lobel, A. (1990). *Alison's Zinnia*. New York: Greenwillow.

Lobel, A. (1979). *Frog and Toad Are Friends*. New York: HarperCollins.

Lobel, A. (1983). *Mouse Soup*. New York: HarperTrophy.

Lobel, A. (1982). *Owl at Home*. New York: HarperTrophy.

MacDonald, S. (1992). *Alphabatics*. New York: Aladdin.

Manushkin, F. (1992). *Latkes and Applesauce*. New York: Scholastic.

Marshall, J. (1996). *Goldilocks and the Three Bears*. New York: Dial.

Martin, B., Jr., (1996). *Brown Bear, Brown Bear, What Do You See?* New York: Holt.

Martin, B., Jr., (1997). *Polar Bear, Polar Bear, What Do You Hear?* New York: Holt.

Martin, B., Jr., & Archambault, J. (1988). *Barn Dance*. New York: Holt.

Martin, B., Jr., & Archambault, J. (1989). *Chicka Chicka Boom Boom*. New York: Simon & Schuster's Children.

Martin, B., Jr., & Archambault, J. (1989). *Here Are My Hands*. New York: Holt.

Martin, B., Jr., & Archambault, J. (1988). *Listen to the Rain*. New York: Holt.

Martin, B., Jr., & Archambault, J. (1991). *Up and Down on the Merry-Go-Round*. New York: Holt.

Marzollo, J. (1994). *Ten Cats Have Hats*. New York: Scholastic.

Marzollo, J., & Wick, W. (1994). *I Spy: A Book of Picture Riddles*. New York: Cartwheel.

Marzollo, J., & Wick, W. (1994). *I Spy Fantasy: A Book of Picture Riddles*. New York: Cartwheel.

Mayer, M. (1982). *Just Me and My Dad*. New York: Golden.

Mayer, M. (1990). *Just Me and My Mom*. New York: Golden.

Mayer, M. (1975). *Just for You*. New York: Golden.

Mayer, M. (1998). *Little Monster Private Goes on Safari*. Scranton, PA: Inchworm.

Mayer, M. (1985). *The New Baby*. New York: Golden.

Mayer, M. (1987). *There's an Alligator under My Bed*. New York: E. P. Dutton.

Mayer, M. (1992). *There's a Nightmare in My Closet*. New York: E. P. Dutton.

Mayer, M. (1987). *What Do You Do with a Kangaroo?* New York: Scholastic.

Mayer, M., & Mayer, M. (1992). *A Boy, a Dog, a Frog, and a Friend*. New York: Dial.

McBratney, S. (1996). *Guess How Much I Love You*. Cambridge, MA: Candlewick.

McCloskey, R. (1976). *Blueberries for Sal*. New York: Viking.

Mcdermott, G. (1987). *Anansi the Spider: A Tale from the Ashanti*. New York: Holt.

McGovern, A. (1997). *The Lady in the Box*. New York: Turtle Books.

McGovern, A. (1987). *Stone Soup*. New York: Scholastic.

McGovern, A. (1992). *Too Much Noise*. Boston: Houghton Mifflin.

McKissack, P. & F. (1985). *Country Mouse and City Mouse*. Chicago: Children's Press.

McKissack, P. C. (1986). *Flossie and the Fox*. New York: E. P. Dutton.

McMullen, K. (1996). *If You Were My Bunny*. New York: Scholastic.

McNaught, H. (1990). *Baby Animals*. New York: Random House.

Melmed, L. K. (1998). *I Love You as Much*. New York: Mulberry.

Modell, F. (1987). *One Zillion Valentines*. New York: William Morrow.

Morris, A. (1993). *Bread Bread Bread*. New York: Mulberry.

Morris, A. (1993). *Hats Hats Hats*. New York: Mulberry.

Morris, A. (1995). *Shoes Shoes Shoes*. New York: Lathrop, Lee & Shepard.

Mosel, A. (1989). *Tikki Tikki Tembo*. New York: Holt.

Most, B. (1996). *Cock-a-Doodle-Moo!* New York: Harcourt Brace.

Most, B. (1990). *The Cow That Went Oink*. New York: Harcourt Brace.

Most, B. (1991). *A Dinosaur Named after Me*. New York: Harcourt Brace.

Munsch, R. (1988). *Love You Forever*. Buffalo, NY: Firefly.

Musgrove, M. (1992). *Ashanti to Zulu: African Traditions*. New York: Dial.

Numeroff, L. (1997). *The Chicken Sisters*. New York: HarperCollins.

Numeroff, L. (1995). *Chimps Don't Wear Glasses*. New York: Simon & Schuster.

Numeroff, L. (1996). *Dogs Don't Wear Sneakers*. New York: Aladdin.

Numeroff, L. (1991). *If You Give a Moose a Muffin*. New York: HarperCollins.

Numeroff, L. (1997). *If You Give a Mouse a Cookie*. New York: HarperTrophy.

Numeroff, L. (1998). *If You Give a Pig a Pancake*. New York: HarperCollins.

Numeroff, L. (1996). *Two for Stew*. New York: Simon & Schuster.

Onyefulu, I. (1997). *A Is for Africa*. New York: Puffin.

Oppenheim, S. L. (1994). *Fireflies for Nathan*. New York: William Morrow.

Otto, C. (1994). *I Can Tell By Touching*. New York: HarperTrophy.

Oxenbury, H. (1981). *Friends*. New York: Little Simon.

Pallotta, J. (1990). *The Bird Alphabet Book*. Watertown, MA: Charlesbridge.

Pallotta, J. (1990). *The Dinosaur Alphabet Book*. Watertown, MA: Charlesbridge.

Pallotta, J. (1989). *The Flower Alphabet Book*. Watertown, MA: Charlesbridge.

Pallotta, J. (1990). *The Frog Alphabet Book*. Watertown, MA: Charlesbridge.

Pallotta, J. (1990). *The Furry Alphabet Book*. Watertown, MA: Charlesbridge.

Pallotta, J. (1993). *The Icky Bug Alphabet Book*. Watertown, MA: Charlesbridge.

Pallotta, J. (1992). *The Icky Bug Counting Book*. Watertown, MA: Charlesbridge.

Pallotta, J. (1990). *The Ocean Alphabet Book*. Watertown, MA: Charlesbridge.

Pallotta, J. (1991). *The Underwater Alphabet Book*. Watertown, MA: Charlesbridge.

Pallotta, J. (1992). *The Victory Garden Alphabet Book*. Watertown, MA: Charlesbridge.

Pallotta, J. (1989). *The Yucky Reptile Alphabet Book*. Watertown, MA: Charlesbridge.

Peet, B. (1987). *Big, Bad Bruce*. Boston: Houghton Mifflin.

Peet, B. (1993). *Cock-a-Doodle Dudley*. Boston: Houghton Mifflin.

Penn, A. (1993). *The Kissing Hand*. Washington, DC: Child Welfare League.

Petersen-Fleming, J., & Fleming, B. (1994). *Puppy Care and Critters, Too!* New York: William Morrow.

Pfeffer, W. (1994). *From Tadpole to Frog*. New York: HarperTrophy.

Pfeffer, W. (1996). *What's It Like to Be a Fish?* New York: HarperTrophy.

Pomerantz, C. (1991). *Where's the Bear?* New York: Mulberry Books.

Potter, B. (1984). *Peter Rabbit*. New York: Viking.

Potter, B. (1984). *The Tale of Jemima Puddle-Duck*. New York: Frederick Warne.

Potter, B. (1987). *The Tale of Squirrel Nutkin*. New York: Frederick Warne.

Pratt, K. J. (1996). *A Fly in the Sky*. Nevada City: Dawn.

Pratt, K. J. (1994). *A Swim through the Sea*. Nevada City: Dawn.

Pratt, K. J. (1992). *A Walk in the Rain Forest*. Nevada City: Dawn.

Prelutsky, J. (1984). *The New Kid on the Block*. New York: Greenwillow Books.

Prelutsky, J. (1983). *The Random House Book of Poetry for Children*. New York: Random House.

Raffi. (1990). *Down by the Bay*. New York: Crown.

Rathman, P. (1994). *Goodnight Gorilla*. New York: Putnam.

Rathman, P. (1995). *Officer Buckle and Gloria*. New York: Putnam.

Reasoner, C. (1989). *Alphabite!: A Funny Feast from A to Z*. Los Angeles: Price Stern Sloan.

Reiser, L. (1994). *Any Kind of Dog*. New York: Mulberry.

Rey, M. & H. A. (1974). *Curious George*. Boston: Houghton Mifflin.

Rey, M. & H. A. (1976). *Curious George Goes to the Hospital*. Boston: Houghton Mifflin.

Rey, M. & H. A. (1973). *Curious George Learns the Alphabet*. Boston: Houghton Mifflin.

Rice, E. (1993). *Benny Bakes a Cake*. New York: Mulberry.

Rojankovsky, F., & Langstaff, J. (1988). *Frog Went A-Courtin'*. New York: Harcourt Brace.

Rosen, M. (1993). *Little Rabbit Foo-Foo*. New York: Aladdin.

Rosen, M. (1997). *We're Going on a Bear Hunt*. New York: Little Simon.

Ross, T. (1992). *Stone Soup*. New York: Dial.

Roy, R. (1990). *Whose Hat is That?* New York: Clarion.

Rylant, C. (1996). *Henry and Mudge: The First Book of Their Adventures*. New York: Aladdin.

Sabuda, R. (1994). *The Christmas Alphabet*. New York: Orchard.

Scamell, R. (1994). *Rooster Crows*. New York: William Morrow.

Schoenherr, J. (1996). *Bear*. New York: Paper Star.

Scieszka, J., & Smith, L. (1998). *The Stinky Cheese Man and Other Fairly Stupid Tales*. New York: Viking.

Seigler, K. (1997). *I'm Going to the Doctor*. Loughborough, Leicestershire, England: Ladybird Books.

Sendak, M. (1962). *Chicken Soup with Rice*. New York: HarperTrophy.

Sendak, M. (1995). *In the Night Kitchen*. New York: HarperTrophy.

Sendak, M. (1991). *Pierre*. New York: HarperTrophy.

Sendak, M. (1988). *Where the Wild Things Are*. New York: HarperTrophy.

Serfozo, M. (1993). *Raintalk*. New York: Aladdin.

Seuss, Dr. (1957). *The Cat in the Hat*. New York: Random House.

Seuss, Dr. (1958). *The Cat in the Hat Comes Back*. New York: Random House.

Seuss, Dr. (1963). *Dr. Seuss's ABC*. New York: Random House.

Seuss, Dr. (1962). *Dr. Seuss's Sleep Book*. New York: Random House.

Seuss, Dr. (1965). *Fox in Socks*. New York: Random House.

Seuss, Dr. (1960). *Green Eggs and Ham*. New York: Random House.

Seuss, Dr. (1966). *Horton Hatches an Egg*. New York: Random House.

Seuss, Dr. (1965). *Horton Hears a Who!* New York: Random House.

Seuss, Dr. (1989). *If I Ran the Zoo*. New York: Random House.

Seuss, Dr. (1981). *One Fish, Two Fish, Red Fish, Blue Fish*. New York: Random House.

Seuss, Dr. (1974). *There's a Wocket in My Pocket*. New York: Random House.

Showers, P. (1991). *How Many Teeth?* New York: HarperCollins.

Silverman, E. (1992). *Big Pumpkin*. New York: Simon & Schuster.

Silverstein, S. (1986). *The Giving Tree*. New York: HarperCollins.

Silverstein, S. (1974). *Where the Sidewalk Ends*. New York: Harper and Row.

Sis, P. (1988). *Waving: A Counting Book*. New York: Greenwillow.

Slate, J. (1996). *Miss Bindergarten Gets Ready for Kindergarten*. New York: Dutton's Children's Books.

Slepian, J., & Seidler, A. (1991). *The Hungry Thing*. New York: Scholastic.

Slobodkina, E. (1987). *Caps for Sale*. New York: HarperTrophy.

Snow, A. (1994). *The Monster Book of ABC Sounds*. New York: Puffin.

So, S. (1998). *C Is for China*. New York: Silver Burdett.

Spier, P. (1993). *The Fox Went Out on a Chilly Night*. New York: Picture Yearling.

Steig, W. (1990). *Doctor De Soto*. New York: Sunburst.

Stewig, J. (1991). *Stone Soup*. New York: Holiday House.

Sturges, P. (1997). *Ten Flashing Fireflies*. New York: North South Books.

Tafuri, N. (1996). *Have You Seen My Duckling?* New York: Greenwillow Books.

Tarsky, S. (1998). *The Busy Building Book*. New York: Putnam.

Tazewell, C. (1982). *The Littlest Angel*. Nashville, TN: Ideals Children's Books.

Tompert, A. (1997). *Grandfather Tang's Story*. Albuquerque, NM: Dragonfly.

Tryon, L. (1994). *Albert's Alphabet*. New York: Aladdin.

Tryon, L. (1996). *Albert's Ballgame*. New York: Macmillan Children's Group.

Tryon, L. (1993). *Albert's Field Trip*. New York: Atheneum.

Tryon, L. (1992). *Albert's Play*. New York: Atheneum.

Van Allsberg, C. (1990). *The Polar Express*. Boston: Houghton Mifflin.

Viorst, J. (1987). *Alexander and the Terrible, Horrible, No Good, Very Bad Day*. New York: Aladdin.

Viorst, J. (1980). *Alexander, Who Used to Be Rich Last Sunday.* New York: Aladdin.

Viorst, J. (1995). *Alexander, Who's Not (Do You Hear Me? I Mean It!) Going to Move.* New York: Atheneum.

Viorst, J. (1997). *Alphabet From Z to A (with Much Confusion on the Way).* New York: Aladdin.

Viorst, J. (1988). *I'll Fix Anthony.* New York: Aladdin.

Viorst, J. (1987). *My Mama Says There Aren't Any Zombies, Ghosts, Vampires, Creatures, Demons, Monsters, Fiends, Goblins or Things.* New York: Aladdin.

Waber, B. (1991). *Bearsie Bear and the Surprise Sleepover.* Boston: Houghton Mifflin.

Waber, B. (1991). *Funny, Funny Lyle.* Boston: Houghton Mifflin.

Waber, B. (1991). *Ira Says Goodbye.* Boston: Houghton Mifflin.

Waber, B. (1979). *Ira Sleeps Over.* Boston: Houghton Mifflin.

Waber, B. (1987). *Lyle, Lyle, Crocodile.* Boston: Houghton Mifflin.

Waddell, M. (1994). *Can't You Sleep Little Bear?* Cambridge, MA: Candlewick.

Waddell, M. (1995). *Let's Go Home Little Bear.* Cambridge, MA: Candlewick.

Waddell, M. (1996). *Owl Babies.* Cambridge, MA: Candlewick.

Waddell, M. (1996). *The Pig in the Pond.* Cambridge, MA: Candlewick.

Waddell, M. (1998). *When the Teddy Bears Came.* Cambridge, MA: Candlewick.

Wallace, J. (1997). *Building a House with Mr. Bumble.* Cambridge, MA: Candlewick.

Walsh E. S. (1995). *Mouse Paint.* San Diego: Red Wagon.

Walton, R. (1996). *How Many, How Many, How Many.* Cambridge, MA: Candlewick.

Watson, W. (1992). *Boo! It's Halloween.* New York: Clarion.

Weiss, N. (1996). *An Egg Is an Egg.* New York: Paper Star.

West, C. (1996). *"I Don't Care!" Said the Bear.* Cambridge, MA: Candlewick.

West, R. (1993). *My Very Own Valentine's Day: A Book of Cooking and Crafts.* Minneapolis: Carolrhoda.

Westcott, N. B. (1988). *I Know an Old Lady Who Swallowed a Fly.* Boston: Little Brown.

Wick, W., & Marzallo, J. (1992). *I Spy Christmas: A Book of Picture Riddles.* New York: Cartwheel.

Williams, S. (1996). *Mommy Doesn't Know My Name.* Boston: Houghton Mifflin.

Wood, A. (1997). *Bird Song.* New York: Harcourt Brace.

Wood, A. (1996). *Elbert's Bad Word.* New York: Harcourt Brace.

Wood, A. (1996). *Heckedy Peg.* New York: Harcourt Brace.

Wood, A. (1985). *King Bidgood's in the Bathtub.* New York: Harcourt Brace.

Wood, A. (1989). *Little Penguin's Tale.* New York: Harcourt Brace.

Wood, A. (1983). *The Napping House.* New York: Harcourt Brace.

Wright, B. F. (1944). *The Real Mother Goose.* New York: Checkerboard Press.

Yee, W. (1995). *A Drop of Rain.* Boston: Houghton Mifflin.

Yolen, J. (1987). *Owl Moon.* New York: Philomel.

Yolen, J. (1996). *Sea Watch: A Book of Poetry.* New York: Philomel.

Young, E. (1995). *Donkey Trouble.* New York: Atheneum.

Young, E. (1994). *I Wish I Were a Butterfly.* New York: Harcourt Brace.

Young, E. (1992). *Seven Blind Mice.* New York: Scholastic.

Zelinsky, P. O. (1990). *The Wheels on the Bus.* New York: E. P. Dutton.

Ziefert, H. (1997). *Eight Days of Hanukkah.* New York: Viking.

Ziefert, H. (1985). *Nicky's Christmas Surprise.* New York: Viking.

Ziefert, H. (1993). *Stitches.* New York: Puffin.

Ziefert, H. (1992). *What Is Halloween?* New York: Harper Festiva.

Ziefert, H., & Taback, S. (1996). *Who Said Moo?* New York: HarperCollins.

Book Share Literacy Focus Index

Note: The numbers shown are Book Share numbers, *not* page numbers.

Book Share Theme Index

Note: The numbers shown are Book Share numbers, *not* page numbers.

Birthday

Food

Gardening

Holidays

Hospital

Nature

New Baby

New Home

Rain

Sleepover

School

Book Share Materials Index

Note: The numbers shown are Book Share numbers, *not* page numbers.

*Appears in more than one category

General Index